Why Classical Music Still Matters

SIMPSON

IMPRINT IN HUMANITIES

The humanities endowment
by Sharon Hanley Simpson and
Barclay Simpson honors
MURIEL CARTER HANLEY
whose intellect and sensitivity
have enriched the many lives
that she has touched.

Why Classical Music Still Matters

Lawrence Kramer

UNIVERSITY OF CALIFORNIA PRESS

Berkeley   Los Angeles   London

University of California Press, one of the most distinguished university presses in the United States, enriches
lives around the world by advancing scholarship in the
humanities, social sciences, and natural sciences. Its activi-
ties are supported by the UC Press Foundation and by phil-
anthropic contributions from individuals and institutions.
For more information, visit www.ucpress.edu.

University of California Press
Berkeley and Los Angeles, California

University of California Press, Ltd.
London, England

Library of Congress Cataloging-in-Publication Data

Kramer, Lawrence, 1946–.
    Why classical music still matters / Lawrence Kramer.
        p.   cm.
    Includes bibliographical references and index.
    ISBN-13: 978-0-520-25803-7 (pbk. : alk. paper)
    1. Music—Philosophy and aesthetics.   I. Title.

ML3800.K72   2007
781.6'8—dc22   2006026454

Manufactured in the United States of America

16   15   14   13   12   11   10   09   08
10   9   8   7   6   5   4   3   2   1

This book is printed on New Leaf EcoBook 50, a 100%
recycled fiber of which 50% is de-inked post-consumer
waste, processed chlorine-free. EcoBook 50 is acid-free and
meets the minimum requirements of ANSI/ASTM D5634-01
(Permanence of Paper).

CONTENTS

IN LIEU OF A PREFACE

What can be done about the state of classical music? In recent years it has sharply declined in popularity and cultural authority; the prospect of its slow disappearance is no longer unthinkable. The music has had advocates, of course, some of them eloquent, but few have asked forthrightly why and how classical music should still matter. That is exactly what this book does. Without pretension or mystification, *Why Classical Music Still Matters* looks for answers that can appeal both to lovers of this music and to skeptics. It describes the sources of the music's power in a wide variety of settings, from concert performance to film and television, from everyday life to the historical trauma of September 11. It affirms the *value* of classical music by revealing what its *values* are: the beliefs, attitudes, and meanings that the music has supported in the past and can support into the future. It shows the traits that make this music distinctive and that offer rich rewards to anyone willing to listen.

The book also clears the air of old prejudices. It refuses to separate classical music from popular culture, or to argue about the superiority or inferiority of musical types, or to accept the idea that special knowledge or guidance is required to enjoy the music. Instead it makes an impassioned but not uncritical case for classical music on the basis of the unique things that the music can be, mean, and do. This is a deeply personal text that nonetheless seeks to argue with rigor and clarity. It is a book that treats classical music from Bach to Tchaikovsky, Chopin to Ligeti, as a living art that still has much to contribute to the art of living.

One practical note. Because it is essayistic—in a sense because it tries to be musical—this book does without footnotes. Citations appear at the end under the rubric "References," keyed to identifying words and phrases from the individual chapters.

CHAPTER ONE

Classical Music and Its Values

Classical music has people worried. To many it seems on shaky ground in America. For more than a decade the drumbeat of its funeral march has been steady. The signs are rife: a wobbly CD market, symphony orchestras struggling to find money and audiences, the press and the Internet fretting over the music's fever chart. The public radio stations that were once the mainstay of classical music broadcasting have been replacing music of any kind with talk, talk, talk. The recording industry is less and less willing to subsidize classical albums for the sake of status and tradition; it has cut back on new recordings and stuffed the "classical" category with treacly high-toned crossover projects that brilliantly manage to combine the worst of both the classical and popular worlds. And classical music is long, long gone from the television networks that once upon a time maintained their own symphony orchestras and broadcast such fare as Leonard Bernstein's Young People's Concerts—in prime time, no less.

You would never guess that fifty years ago the music was flourishing on the strength of a recent invention, the long-playing record, which made it more available than ever before. You would never guess that a hundred years ago it was the hottest thing going on the cultural scene. People longed for it, argued about it, swooned over it. In those days you heard it live and hot or not at all, and no one had to worry about that musty "classical" label we're now stuck with. The echoes of that musical world were still audible when I was a teenager in New York City in the early 1960s. Some of my most vivid memories of the time involve summer nights in a stadium filled with people from all walks of life, from all over the city. The acoustics were terrible; the pleasure was overflowing; the ovations were long and noisy.

Free concerts in New York's Central Park can still draw crowds, but the cultural atmosphere has distinctly changed. No wonder that when one classical music lover meets another, each heaves a silent sigh of relief: the fear that the music will become extinct creeps down a notch.

The danger of extinction can be exaggerated by these anxious fans. There are statistics that tell a happier story—healthy Internet downloads and a robust increase in concert offerings over earlier decades, with audiences to match. But the feeling of danger is itself a fact to be reckoned with. Something still feels wrong; something still *is* wrong. The problem is perhaps less economic or demographic than it is cultural, less a question of the music's survival than of its role. A small cohort of the population (and it was never much more) may still favor classical music, but the music does not mean what it once did. For what it's worth, my anecdotal impression is that people are generally less knowledgeable about it than they were even a generation ago. People still listen, but the days when listening to classical music could feel like an integral part of cultural life are long gone. We know, some of us, how to enjoy it, but we don't know what to do with it. In this sense, classical music is indeed on shaky ground in America.

One reason why is the loss of a credible way to maintain that people *ought* to listen to this music, that the music is something that should not be missed. Our growing reluctance to impose prescriptive or judgmental *should*s has obscured the power of the *should* that says, "Don't deprive yourself of this pleasure, this astonishment, this conception!" If you don't listen, no one is supposed to mind. No wonder, then, that many culturally literate people who visit museum exhibits and keep up with the latest books, movies, and ideas think nothing of being classical-music illiterates. There is nothing, any more, that one just has to hear.

Meanwhile, the music industry relentlessly pushes its more profitable products out into a soundtracked world where they can't help being heard. Music in general becomes something to get excited about but not to take too seriously. Status accrues, not to music, but to its performers. Bands and singers become temporary demigods and permanent media fodder, their charisma and celebrity usurping the luminosity that music once claimed as its own. Lovers of popular music aren't always gratified by this; many are well aware that "product" tends to be more important than creativity. But the product is what there is. For many people in the first years of the third millennium, the supposedly timeless body of classical music is just irrelevant.

For me it is anything but. I not only love this music but also make my career as an academic writing about it. Like many in both positions, I've often wondered what, if anything, people like me can do to help fix things.

Two efforts, it's seemed very clear, could certainly help make things worse. The first would be to explain patiently that if people would only absorb some technical information, follow the instructions of an expert, and listen for some formal routines, they could come to understand this music and discover that it is not only "great" but also good for them. Virgil Thomson long ago skewered this approach as the "music-appreciation racket." The second bad choice is to try hectoring people into the belief that this music really is good for them by praising it and its composers in extravagantly high-minded terms and generally suggesting that the best people like the best music. The first attitude is condescending and authoritarian, the second pompous and moralistic. If I felt that classical music really supported such attitudes—or rather, needed to support them, since the attitudes themselves have been all too common—I too would run for the nearest exit.

What, then, can someone like me do to help? Well, maybe nothing, but I don't want to believe that. This book is my version of "maybe something; maybe this." It springs from an effort to shed both my long-accustomed assumptions and my professional interests to ask for a simple answer to a simple question: What's in this music for me? In other words, why does classical music still matter?

I like listening to it, of course, but I like listening to some other kinds of music too. With classical music I also like to eavesdrop on myself, to listen in on my own experience. I feel impelled to think about what the music demands and what it offers, what visions it summons and what logic it pursues. These and similar questions seem inseparable from the music, which poses them in the very act of capturing attention and giving pleasure. And they are questions with a wider resonance. This music provides as much insight as it invites; thinking and writing about it gives me a means of pondering big questions of culture, history, identity, desire, and meaning. The music is full of powerful feelings, but they're feelings that are always pushing beyond their own boundaries to open and refresh these questions. This music stimulates my imagination and my speculative energies while it sharpens my senses and quickens my sense of experience.

Of course all music, whatever its type, is a gift to its devotees. Music enhances life; almost everyone loves some form of it. The real question about classical music is not whether it rewards our attention but how it does—the very thing I've only just begun to suggest. Its rewards, I'm convinced, have nothing to do with the elitism and esotericism too often associated with this music. They are accessible to anyone with open ears and a sense of adventure; they require no mysterious rites of initiation. To find them out it is necessary only to talk about musical experience with confidence and precision.

Here classical music may have a certain advantage in the rich vocabulary available to describe it. This music has historically maintained a prolific dialogue with language, even though, like all music, it is supposed to work, and does work, at levels above or below language, even when the music, being sung, uses language with great expressive power. One of the most remarkable features of classical music is the way it always seems to teeter on the edge of speech. We can never know just what it—almost—says, but we can harmonize our words with its sounds in ways worth hearing.

That's what this book tries to do. My idea for it was to identify some of the distinctive life-enhancing qualities of classical music by using language freely to show them in action. By presenting an example of how one listener enters into a kind of intimate dialogue with this music, its history, and its values, I might be able to suggest to others that the music really is worth bothering about. Those who already believe in its value might find that the resources of their own dialogues can expand in gratifying, perhaps unexpected ways. At the very least the question could be raised afresh among both the music's friends and its foes. A fresh airing is just what we need at this point. So I decided to share some of my own musical dialogue, built up of listening, thinking, writing, and a bit of lore: not in raw form, of course, but shaped and elaborated to bring out its hidden consistencies, including consistencies previously hidden from the author.

No hectoring, no lectures, no pretense of instruction from on high: just a record of lived and living experience that might strike a chord with the experience of others. The idea is simply to suggest by example how classical music can become a source of pleasure, discovery, and reflection tuned not only to the world of the music, rich though that is, but also to the even richer world beyond the music.

This project involves some risks, including preachiness and pretentiousness. It's pretty awkward when academics pretend to shed their robes to seek a wider audience and end up doing justice neither to the audience they seek nor to their academic friends. But risks, like learning, go with any venture worth trying. So, though mindful of the fabled astronomer who fell in the ditch while looking at the stars, I will trust that my steps have better instincts and hope for an unmuddy outcome.

As an academic, I can imagine several other problems that need to be faced at the outset. These musical remarks, someone is sure to say, are arbitrary, merely subjective, untrustworthy as knowledge of anything but my whims. Besides, the remarks don't rise much above the level of—dread term!—program notes. They don't go deep enough because you can't go deeply into music without getting into questions of technique that only experts can deal with.

To these imagined charges, I cheerfully plead a qualified "guilty." Art, being formed from imagination and addressed to the imagination, needs to be answered imaginatively. Some learning, of course, is involved; no one's imagination benefits from ignorance. But responses to art neither can nor should be verifiable, only credible, and they achieve credibility by a lucky combination of knowledge, insight, and a feel for playing hunches. Interpretation may inevitably be subjective, but subjectivity is neither arbitrary nor whimsical. We have to learn subjectivity, be taught how to have it and practice it: much of subjectivity is in the public domain. And an idea that begins subjectively does not have to end that way. It can and should be tested, discussed, submitted to evidence, examined for reasonableness. The notion that we can keep reason and imagination in separate compartments, separate cages, does a great disservice to both.

As for the program note, it's a fine institution if by it one means a few words offering curious listeners an angle at which to cock their ears, a device to fine-tune their hearing. My remarks do aim to do this. They dwell on what anyone can hear and ask how to hear it well. But they are more conceptually ambitious than most program notes and less wedded to the mystique of musical form. In them I try to reflect both on and with music in contexts abuzz with matters of general importance. And I go into technical detail, with minimal jargon, only far enough to connect the formal language of music with significant measures of pleasure and understanding.

One of the implicit points of this book is that a little such observation can go a long way.

This is not to deny that a lot can go a long way too. I'm trying to write nonacademically here, not antiacademically. But music does not communicate esoterically, or, if it does, it ceases to communicate at all. There is no reason to feel that you don't really understand it if you don't know the code. Musical meaning does not depend on being decoded; it depends on being lived. My remarks here are addressed neither to experts nor to nonexperts but just to you, whoever you are, holding this book and reading these lines because something about the topic matters to you.

If classical music doesn't make sense at this level of human interest, the other, supposedly deeper layers just don't matter much, at least to me. I want to reject the idea that there's a deep musical truth that loose talk about meaning and expression obscures and dumbs down. The meaning and expression are what matters; the rest should just be a way of showing how and why in more detail to those who find the detail compelling. (I do, of course; that's why I write about music for a living.) My aim in this book is to encourage an activity that nonprofessionals think they can't do and professionals feel they shouldn't do. I want to encourage doing things with classical music so that classical music can do things for us. That, even more than the content of my statements—and I care plenty about the content—is the heart of this project.

But how to keep this heart beating? I don't want to string together random musical remarks, but neither do I want to be systematic or professorial. And I want to be able to speak personally at times while also making use of such knowledge as I may have. My problem, in fact, is one I share with classical music itself. How do you reconcile richness of detail with a guiding thread? How do you find your way, enjoy the passage, and avoid the Minotaur?

My solution here is to keep this book focused on indispensable human concerns, the stuff of real life. Music may sometimes offer us needed relief from life's burdens, but it serves us better, I believe, when it offers us insight, intuition, and empathy. My topics are memory, ecstasy, identity, and war; they are suffering and longing, solitude and community, love and death. I write about these things through classical music—write about them *because* I am writing about this music, and write with the understanding that the music both draws meaning from them and imparts meaning to them.

These topics arise not as abstractions or generic themes but as concrete, historically specific matters of importance that find some of their many voices in this music. Sometimes what these voices convey is challenging; although I always aim to write clearly, I trust the reader to accompany me through the occasional rough patch. There are not many of them. My effort involves stories about how particular works of music can draw the listener into a vital dialogue that is the very opposite of recondite or rarefied. It asks what such music has made it possible to hear and to heed. It seeks to bring out the distinctive alliance of listening, subjective enrichment, and social participation basic to classical music. With no apologies, it treats this music as a gateway to the experience of a primal sympathy between sentience and sound.

The role of classical music in movies is prominent in this book; no modern medium has influenced the history of listening more than the cinema, which is also the locale where classical music today, if only in bits and pieces, finds its largest audience. The role of performance is prominent, too, since classical music comes into being in the passage from a written score to a sounding performance—a simple and obvious journey that is neither simple nor obvious. But because for most people enjoying music no longer means knowing how to play it, the experience of music making remains in the background. Or rather it acts from the background. I find both a model and an inspiration for this project in my own eager but maladroit piano playing. Like such playing, listening to classical music involves both unselfconscious absorption in the sweep of a piece as a whole and quickened attention to special details. This wavering balance holds the key both to my way of proceeding in this book and to the beliefs that underlie it.

The results are anything but exhaustive. Many composers and compositions I value greatly never come up. They don't have to. The idea is to evoke a frame of reference and a frame of mind in which they might have, in which they might yet, as compellingly as a tune that pops unbidden into your head. My hope is that by doing this I can suggest the wider power of resonance—of sound, thought, feeling, belief, and value—that constitutes the enduring relevance of classical music.

That power comes from the discovery, the development, and the dissemination of a special type of listening. Music is never simply heard; it comes to us through practices of listening that help form our sense of the world. Classical music is a pivotal event in the history of listening, a history that it in part makes possible. Its impact on how we listen, what we listen for, and with what significance will take this whole book to unfold. Meanwhile it is important to be clear about just what prompts this listening. When I speak of classical music here I am not using the catchall commercial category that takes in some six centuries of very diverse practice, including opera, a theatrical genre with its own quite different set of problems and values. For purposes of this book, the term *classical music* refers to a specific body of nontheatrical music produced since the eighteenth century with one aim in view: to be listened to.

Or perhaps we should say to be listened *into*. All music trains the ear to hear it properly, but classical music trains the ear to hear with a peculiar acuity. It wants to be explored, not just heard. It "trains" the ear in the sense of pointing, seeking: it trains both the body's ear and the mind's to hearken, to attend closely, to listen deeply, as one wants to listen to something not to be missed: a secret disclosed, a voice that enchants or warns or soothes or understands, a faint echo of the music traditionally said to hold the world itself together in a kind of harmony.

This kind of listening is done not with the ear but with the whole person. It is not the result of learning a technique (the stuff of the "music-appreciation racket") but of adopting an attitude. It is not a passive submission to the music but an active engagement with it, a meeting of our ability to become absorbed—sometimes for just a few moments or even less, sometimes for hours on end— with the music's capacity to absorb us. In attending to classical music, we also *tend* it: we tend to it and tend toward it, we adopt and argue with its way of moving and being. We dwell on it by dwelling in it. We don't simply realize something *about* it; we *realize* the music in a more primary sense: we give it realization, as one realizes a plan or vision or a desire. Such listening is even a mental equivalent to the performance of the music as the performer might feel it while making expressive decisions, shaping, phrasing, pacing, emphasizing, hiding, revealing, conveying. Classical music performance is also a practice of listening.

Such listening is perhaps particularly important at this historical moment, the very moment that seems to be most in danger of losing it. In a world that moves at digital speed, a world increasingly crowded by people, ideas, and agendas, a maelstrom of technological change, ecological danger, and cultural conflicts that are often virulent even when they manage, ever more narrowly, to avoid violence, the ability to listen deeply, to open the labyrinths of the ear and be sounded out by the voices that address us, may be the very ability we want the most.

Want in both senses: lack and desire. This want shows up revealingly in connection with another of classical music's present troubles. It is often said that the music is fading because contemporary composers have lost or spurned their audiences and left only a museum culture behind, something that may be monumental but that, like any monument, is the sign of something dead. The complaint about contemporary composition has some truth to it, although not the whole truth; today's classical scene is full of moving and exciting new music, some of which we will touch on. But the museum metaphor is misguided. It gives too little credit to museums. Classical music should only be so lucky as to have a museum culture. Museums have become more popular than ever just as classical music has been floundering.

This is a result partly of clever marketing, but partly of the discovery that museums can offer a space that permits cultivation without requiring stuffiness. Unlike the traditional concert hall, the museum has become an animated space by affording opportunities to combine sociability, informality, and the enjoyment of art. Concert producers sorely need to find a way to do the same. But beyond these incitements, the museum has become a desirable space precisely because it is shaped for unhurried reflection in a world where unhurried reflection is the rarest of commodities. It is a space outside the hurly-burly of the world from which it is possible, in imagination, in fantasy, in symbol, to reconstitute the world in relation to human desire. The art on exhibit may be tragic, ironic, even brutal, without interdicting this temporary world-making. But it would be disingenuous to deny that another thing museums do is exhibit art that preserves the traditional measures of human desire side by side with the images of tragedy and brutality. So in a certain sense the museum is not only a space of world-making but an institution of human hope.

Classical music, I would like to say, is the same kind of thing: a living museum, living precisely because it is a kind of museum, and, like a museum, a place that exhibits new works as well as old. But just as the museum focuses the eye not only through the art seen but through the ways of seeing that the museum affords, so classical music trains the ear to hearken not only through the music heard but through the ways of listening that the music institutes.

A concern for the values made available by attentive listening and threatened by its erosion in contemporary society is something I share with another recent writer on this topic. The writer, as it happens, is British—proof that the malaise of classical music is not just an American problem. In *Who Needs Classical Music?* Julian Johnson invokes the traditional distinction between art and entertainment to argue that classical music, music as art, is something we all need. Such music distances us from the distracting immediacy of everyday life. It gives us a vision of authentic subjectivity. Listening to its quasi-autonomous unfolding thus becomes both a social act and an ethical act. It is a social act in that it resists the relentless pressures of consumerism and the culture industry, the bread and circuses of the contemporary world. It is an ethical act in that it enables us to affirm our humanity more fully against the ideological and economic administration of our lives by forces that do not govern us by our true consent. Johnson is not averse to saying that classical music is redemptive. Listened to closely, its form gives us an ideal vision of what we may be.

I have no wish to quarrel with this position. Part of me is in sympathy with it. But part of me is disturbed by its implicit revival of the idea that an absorption in high culture, "the best that has been thought and said," can make us better people. I do not think that classical music has a patent on authenticity or idealism or an immunity from practical interests. Nor do I think that music, any music, can redemptively disentangle us from our worldly destinies. Its power, rather, is to entangle us with those destinies in ways that can be profoundly important.

Classical music is exceptionally good at this for the very reasons that Johnson and many others think it does the contrary. This music does draw close attention to the course of its unfolding; it does insist on its own presence above and beyond the event of its performance and the force of its expression. But in doing so classical music draws closer to the texture of experience, not further away from it. Just how this happens we will hear as this book unfolds. Suffice it for now to say that although becoming absorbed in the logic and play, the movement and the texture, of this music offers extraordinary possibilities of pleasure, this absorption does not involve ignoring everything but the music. It does not foster what has sometimes been called "structural listening," either as an ideal or as a practical likelihood. We always listen with worldly ears, enveloped with fragments of language, imagery, memory, and fantasy that embed this music, and any music, in the very world from which we've been told to think of it as abstracted and told we're not listening well unless we think so.

We've been told wrong. For most of the nineteenth century, classical music gave most of its listeners what felt like open access to the life of feeling. For part of the twentieth century, it continued to do so to ever-widening audiences created by the development of radio and sound recording—which, however, also created the mass audience for popular music. Caught out by a formidable rival on one hand and a loss of participants on the other, classical music lost part of its emotional transparency as the century progressed. Music that once seemed utterly available now seemed to harbor secrets. Newly composed music became harder to hear, more, perhaps, because of this change in aural perspective than because some modern music (though by no means all) is difficult. A defensive reaction was inevitable. After a while, the friends of classical music began to take cultural isolation as its natural and desirable condition. Listening to it gradually turned from something that anyone could do enjoyably into a disciplined procedure that required training by experts.

These developments were not entirely negative. They spurred musical innovation and encouraged hard thinking about musical aesthetics and musical form. Their net effect, however, was damaging and alienating. The culture of classical music came to seem, not without justice, mandarin and out of touch, ripe for obsolescence. As I said at the start, my motive in this book is to give a tug in the other direction. The energies of this music are still vital; its value is still inestimable. The trick is to unlock the energies and recover the value. What's needed for that is a way to refresh listening: to reconnect the listener with a community and culture of listening, and to do so as far as possible without anxiety or defensiveness.

One proof that this project is not merely quixotic came amid the shock and horror following the events of September 11, 2001. For many people trying to come to terms with the cataclysm, classical music provided a perhaps unexpected, perhaps momentary, but nonetheless real resource, consoling in both an emotional and something like a metaphysical sense. And also a communal sense, for this was a matter not just of listening but of listening together—something that recording technologies often obscure but that all listening ought in some sense to be. In New York the Philharmonic gave a benefit concert featuring Brahms's *German Requiem*; the Metropolitan Opera staged a benefit performance of segments from three Verdi operas and projected it onto an outdoor screen overlooking the plaza at Lincoln Center.

Such music proliferated around the country. In New Orleans, for example, as reported by the *New York Times*:

> The [Louisiana Philharmonic] is trying to help people deal with the jumble of emotions that welled up after this month's stunning wave of terror. At its opening night concert, just two days after the attacks on New York and Washington, the program was changed to include the contemplative adagio movement of Beethoven's Symphony no. 9.

Over the days that followed, members of the orchestra formed small groups to play in lobbies of office buildings. They distributed copies of a statement pledging "to redouble our effort to keep beauty and harmony and music in our beloved community."

Crowds of people stopped to watch and listen. Tears glistened in more than a few eyes.

"When people left our opening night concert, you could see they had shed so much of their weight," [said Sharon Litwin, the orchestra's executive director]. . . . "I think everyone who heard our musicians this week came away with a deep appreciation for the intrinsic power of music. It did what music is supposed to do: it touched your soul, it soothed, it calmed."

Music, of course, is supposed to do more than soothe and calm. There are also those *other* three movements of Beethoven's Ninth, full of violence, exuberance, and rapture. But the language of "beauty and harmony" was what people needed in these difficult weeks, and music, in this case classical music above all, could justify that language and seem to speak it. The "intrinsic power" of this music was not the specific power to soothe and calm but the power to do what music is supposed to do, precisely that, whatever it may be: to give what is needed, give what is asked for, without qualification or stint. The music, in doing that, gave not only consolation but also the sense of community without which the consolation itself would scarcely have been possible.

This perhaps explains part of my own experience at the time. I found it impossible to listen to music (any music, really, but I mean classical music) in isolation; the CD player in my study was silenced. Without support from fellow listeners, I found the very consolations of the music, the architecture of sound, the channeling of energy, the spectrum of goodhearted feelings, almost impossible to bear. They seemed discredited, rendered glib and foolish by the enormity of events.

There is something to be said for this impression, as there is something to be said for the critical, questioning, obstreperous side of the music to which I was temporarily deaf and that the darkness of the time had made it necessary to put in abeyance. At some time I would need to ask music to give that back, not as a way of opposing the effects of beauty and harmony but as a way of securing them, justifying them, making them credible again. For the time being, the best I could do on my own was not to listen passively but to listen at the piano, listen by playing: playing, as I usually do, pieces a shade or two harder than I can play well, or at full tempo, or with full confidence. As long as I had to struggle to grasp the music in an affirmative spirit, the spirit would not wholly elude my grasp. Perhaps it was the shared element of struggle that made listening in the company of others so powerful a source of solace in the time of crisis.

But just what is it that this listening heeded? What makes classical music the special thing I claim it is? The remainder of this first chapter is devoted to these questions. It will suggest some answers by looking first more closely at focused listening, then at the nature and meaning of classical composition, and finally at the emotional makeup of classical music. These considerations will bring us to some preliminary conclusions that the book as a whole will test and develop.

As I said earlier, classical music developed with a single aim: to be listened to. Listened to, that is, rather than heard as part of some other activity, usually a social or religious ritual. As noted earlier, too, this sort of listening involves both focused attention and active involvement. Its attention is a form of attending; it is not just a hearing but a hearkening. To practice it is to presuppose that listening is a discrete form of activity, of interest in itself independent of what is heard. Listening so conceived is capable of sustaining personal, social, and spiritual values depending on how it goes, and when, and for whom. Such listening quickly develops the ambition to get beyond the quicksilver transitory character of hearing in the moment. It seeks to embody itself in forms that can endure and so become the "classics" on which a culture of heightened listening depends.

Classical music invented listening in this sense. The invention went along with the eighteenth century's epoch-making concern with freedom of thought and feeling. It flourished along with the political and philosophical "discovery" that human beings are grounded in deep inner selves, that each of us has a private core of being to call our own. This inner person is important in a host of ways. It is as that person that I have mental freedom, political liberty, and human rights. It is the inner self that guarantees our uniqueness to each of us; it is the basis of identity in the modern world. Most important for present purposes, when we listen intently to music, it is the inner self that hears.

The experience of this inner self defines the sphere of subjectivity. The term has already come up in the everyday sense that refers to personal belief and sensation as opposed to fact. But *subjectivity* may also be used to designate the full range of mental and physical states that compose the inner life of human beings. The person understood in relation to subjectivity in this sense is accordingly termed the subject. It will often be necessary to refer to subjects and subjectivity, their qualities and their histories, in this book because music is directly concerned with them. One way to grasp the singularity of classical music is to understand how it addresses, and influences, and expresses subjects and their subjectivities.

We might as well start now. A key feature of the modern subject—the modern person with an inner self—is that the inner core of self is both absolutely one's own and yet mysterious. We know it better than anything else, yet it defies full understanding. By heightened listening, or so people came to feel, that remote and mysterious inner being could be brought to life and both enjoyed and comprehended. Classical music was in part devised for that purpose. When we enjoin someone to "listen" to an utterance—that is, to heed it—we usually think of the message conveyed by its words. What classical music helped its listeners to discover was that the act of listening intently could become both meaningful in its own right and a source of wider meaning. There is, or so the music made people feel, a truth in listening that touches on the fundamental truths of subjective existence. The listening may in part have created the depths it was felt to reveal, but that it could do so, that music could do so, was a remarkable discovery in its own right.

This is the music of the self that Jean-Jacques Rousseau, a sometime musician as well as a philosopher, proclaimed on the first page of his *Confessions* of 1764: "The man I portray will be myself. Simply myself. I know my own heart and understand my fellow man. But I am made unlike anyone I have ever met." This is the music sought out by such a self when, rich in feeling but baffled by some inner enigma, it needs to grasp itself as a whole, however fleetingly. This is the music, too, of the self invoked in Kant's majestic formulation of the moral law as a categorical imperative: "Act in such a way that you always treat humanity, whether in your own person or in the person of another, never simply as a means, but always at the same time as an end."

The modern subject addressed by this music experiences its divided existence as exhilarating in some respects, disturbing in others. How could it do otherwise? This ambivalence is as fundamental a part of the modern self-concept as the ideas of freedom, authenticity, and depth. The subject achieves its rich inner life only in return for a surrender of full self-knowledge. The exchange brings a self-estrangement that has to be embraced rather than resisted, a task, to put it mildly, that is not always easy. The luminosity of the inner self somewhere contains a hard nub of opacity, a kind of inner sunspot. This darkness on the core provokes constant symbolization while eluding all final determination by symbol, law, or force. In its positive guise, this inner excess is felt as a continual refreshment of the sense of identity, a reservoir of meaningful being; its darkness is fecund. In its negative guise, the same excess harbors the darkness of enigma. It continually troubles, disturbs, betrays, and deceives us and distorts our perception of ourselves and others.

Classical music involves both the rewards and the risks of this model, which it does not merely reflect but historically helped create, support, and develop. In part the fortunes of the music are staked on the fortunes of this self-concept. And the concept is hardly without its faults and mutations. People today may no longer be automatically guided by it, either because they regard it as out of date or because they feel that the conditions of contemporary life make it unattainable. Yet as long as people are susceptible to the ideal of a free, rich subjectivity, as long as they feel that this subjectivity has a dimension of depth that, if plumbed, can yield both pleasure and knowledge, the music will retain the power to move and enlighten them. It may even retain the power to frighten and disturb, to speak to and for the parts of our subjectivity we cannot hope to command or master. For that, too, it should be welcome. The ideas behind this music still have life in them, a life by turns surprising, reassuring, nostalgic, and uncanny. Even at the dawn of an era in which information technology threatens many of their core assumptions, even in the bleak light of an era in which civic and intellectual liberties are under mounting siege worldwide, these ideas continue to pervade the way we think and speak about people and societies.

We might say, then, that the gift of classical music is listening itself. The music attuned itself to previously unheard and unheard-of potentialities of listening and made them available to be given. The recipient is the modern self, which has to listen differently, as it has to live differently, from its forebears. This music gives subjectivity ears. The next step is to ask what they listen to.

Classical music differs from many other kinds in being fully composed. In most pieces, allowing for limited, historically specific exceptions (the figured bass, the concerto cadenza), every detail of design has been attended to. Every pitch, rhythm, and instrumental color is predetermined and notated. As a result, the details tend to do far more than support and enrich an expressive totality. In the course of doing that (and sometimes undoing it), they act out independent dramas, form rivalries, find and lose meanings, pursue affinities and antagonisms. Everything that happens, even the smallest thing, can matter, and matter a lot. Details add up to processes that take on a life of their own under the broad umbrella of the whole.

This is not to say either that everything matters equally in classical pieces or that details in other genres are insignificant. Details in fully composed music vary greatly in their dramatic force and depth of implication. They vary both with the design of a piece and with the understanding on which a piece is heard. Improvised or partly composed music may also be rich in important details, but with a difference. With jazz improvisation, say, or popular song, the referent of the details is a particular performance or recording rather than an ideal object projected through notation. Songs are written to be arranged and rearranged at will, and they don't lose their essential identity no matter what a performer does with them. Jazz improvisation, like classical composition, is, on the contrary, committed to uniqueness, but the uniqueness is that of an occasion, a specific exercise of creative energy that can be reheard but never reexperienced in its original form.

Classical pieces have no "original" form. They cannot be represented by the event of any single performance. They are, as I said, ideal objects, approximately realized through repeated performances that may vary widely in some respects but must still respect the limits imposed by the score. This description, of course, is itself ideal. The exact meaning of its mandate has varied over time. The rule of realization does not apply to transcriptions and arrangements on the one hand or to many avant-garde experiments on the other, and it is complicated by scores in different versions and editions and by the former practice of "retouching" orchestration. But every time a classical piece is played from score, the ideal is reinstated. Any performance from score realizes—performs—the ideal as well as the music. In a perfectly literally sense, a classical composition is one that we can listen to repeatedly but never actually hear.

The disparity between the performance or recording of a classical piece and its purely ideal or virtual existence is not just a neutral or theoretically interesting fact. It actively affects the experience of listening by creating a metaphorical space that the music and the listener can occupy together. Because we always hear the music in transition between its ideal and its actual sound, everything we hear is full of a specific potentiality that the music makes actual as it goes along. The details of classical music are composed to be heard in this environment, where they are highly exposed. They enter into highly articulated dramas, scenarios, processes, rituals, and the like, lines of musical action that return with each new performance to be reinterpreted by both the players and the listener. Music that has a "real" existence because it is partly composed in being performed affects us differently. Its most salient details are not interpretations but creative interventions meant to sustain or diversify a compelling musical effect. These are the details that complete the music through its performance. Classical music cannot be completed in the same way; it cannot really be completed at all.

This incompletion is a creative medium, and the details that animate classical music thrive on it. They do not assume their significance as elements of form, and even less as the fine points to be noticed by a refined taste. They act as what Wallace Stevens called parts of a world. They are occasions of insight, understanding, pleasure, feeling, and even revelation that come, and come often, to the attentive listener or absorbed performer, to the one who hearkens. As one adopts an attitude of openness toward the music, the music opens to the possibilities of experience and expression. Its details assume a luminosity drawn from and extending to the full texture of experience. The meanings that thus become perceptible are not somehow contained in the music or simply revealed by it. They are made available to, and by, the listening subject, who must in part create them to experience them. The music offers the opportunity to shape the activity of listening in the current and contour of such meanings, to take pleasure and find insight in a rendition of the texture of our historical being.

It is this process, I believe, and not the traditional retinue of aesthetic criteria—unity, structure, coherence, complexity, formal or narrative tension and resolution—that accounts for the power and durability of classical pieces and repertoires. Many forgotten or little-esteemed works meet all the criteria with little or no effect. The truth is that meeting aesthetic criteria is easy. Many much-beloved works do not bother to do it, or do it as a matter of routine while going about their more vital business. I am working here toward a different ideal, one based on the belief that something distinctive and particular, something arresting in its special and often unforeseen pertinence, must happen in, through, by, or about a piece of music to make it live.

The detail that matters may or may not take part in some grand aesthetic synthesis, but the synthesis is itself only another sort of detail. It is neither the reason the detail matters nor, above all, the thing that really matters about the detail. Musical detail matters because it animates the details of which our lives—our lives in particular, not in general—are made. Classical music makes this process its deepest concern.

Of course neither this music nor any other has some kind of simple one-to-one relationship to experience, any more than it has a simple one-to-one relationship with the words through which we describe it. Musical meaning comes about when a spark leaps up between some musical detail and an idea or image, a metaphor or turn of phrase, a movement or a gesture, a perception or a memory. It does not matter whether this process starts or ends with the music, whether it occurs when we respond to the music we hear or when we respond with music to some other thing. Either way, we bring the music close to some worldly circumstance in the faith that the closeness is something recognized, not something concocted. The meanings that arise in this proximity belong to the music as much as to the circumstances; they are both made and discovered at the same time. The music is their matrix of possibility. It is a kind of antechamber in which they wait to be realized, to become what they are.

We can illustrate this mysterious but immediately felt process in the way two recent films deal with the same work, the Prelude to Johann Sebastian Bach's Suite for Unaccompanied Cello in G Major. This is music of great lyric energy that combines the strength of the cello's sonority with the fragility of a solitary utterance. It flows continuously, connecting spacious arpeggios—chords played as if on a harp, one note at a time, in rising, falling, or wavelike patterns—with runs of increasing breadth and animation. The primary common chords, the tonic and dominant, evoke a sense of acoustic space that the music fills and fills until it brims over.

In *Master and Commander: The Far Side of the World* (2003), a naval saga of the Napoleonic wars, the Prelude forms an evocation of unspoiled, undiscovered nature. The scene is the Galapagos Islands, where (as we know, but the characters do not) Charles Darwin will voyage a few years later on the *Beagle* and find the pageant of evolution unrolling before his eyes.

Heard twice nearly in its entirety, the Prelude anticipates the thrill of that discovery in a manner far removed from the infa-

mous "nature red in tooth and claw"—and from the violence of
the battles at sea to which the island stopover is merely an interlude. The music's proliferation of arpeggios and scales conveys
the prolific vitality of nature, the thrill of evolutionary movement as embodied in the sight of aquatic birds and mammals at
their gambols, the utterly benign proliferation (or so it seems,
here in this island paradise) of living forms. The music evolves
like nature and flows like water. It represents a mode of singularity that transcends the delicate, uncertain balance represented by
the violin-cello duets played elsewhere in the narrative by the
friends, the ship's captain and ship's doctor, who are its heroes.
The duets are Mozart transcriptions in which the give-and-take
of the instrumental voices can almost, but not quite, reconcile
the conflicting agendas of a man of science and a man of war.

The Pianist (2002) retells the true story of the Polish pianist
Wladic Szpilman, a Jew who survived the Holocaust by a combination of sheer chance and the kindness of strangers. Hiding
from the Nazis in the apartment of a cellist friend and her husband, he wakes one morning to the disembodied sounds of the
G-Major Prelude. As he, and we, discover his friend playing the
piece to herself in another room, the music appears introspec-
tive, withdrawn. It sounds like a solitary effort to hold the self
together for a few extra moments before the world falls apart.

But the effort is not exactly solitary. The cellist is pregnant; to
play the Prelude for herself is also to wrap her unborn child in its
resonance on the instrument as close to her womb as the child is.
The music's contemplative energy, tranquility set in motion,
becomes the sign of a maternal and cultural symbiosis that is
both eternal and fragile. We can see as well as hear these qualities when Szpilman first awakens and the camera tracks his gaze

to a flower-filled vase of glass, symbolically set at the center of a table. Here the exaltation of common chords does not so much embody the harmony of nature as create a safe cultural space, a haven like the mother's body for the child. The music forms a metaphorical safe house doubling the literal ones where Szpilman takes refuge. It is, not by chance, a remnant of Germany's cultural heritage that the Nazis have not yet succeeded in corrupting, or so the film asks us to believe. The Prelude is the only place left in which it is still possible to believe in beauty, in culture, in the future, while atrocity rages outside.

In their use of this music, these films provide a model of creative listening, listening with both music and meaning in mind. The films realize the meanings that lie like seeds in the music, eager to be disseminated. All it takes to release them is the "application" of the music to the dramatic situation. In this case the effect extends to the composer as well as to the music. The films continue a long tradition of treating Bach as "classical," which is strictly speaking an anachronism. (We will return to this point late in the book, where the Bach G-Major Suite will meet us again in a similar context.) The point to dwell on here is the power of this anachronism to support, to merge with, both emotional and conceptual truths: to make its own fiction a kind of truth.

The results are vivid because they are utterly concrete. But their concreteness should mislead no one; its creation is confined neither to these films nor to the film medium. *Master and Commander* and *The Pianist* simply do what anyone can do, and do without necessarily invoking a specific story or a specific image. Anyone can hear the force of vital proliferation in the Bach suite, the energy of nature sounding and resounding in the elaboration of the common chords and their majestic final return. And anyone can hear the quality of introspection in the same music, the thoughtful reconsideration of phrases and ideas in a continuous flow both powerful and fragile. All we have to do is trust our ears and our words, knowing that they derive their authority from the dialogue between an inevitably creative intelligence and an inevitably meaningful world.

We might say, then, that when we listen creatively to a classical work, as these films do, we travel in a long arc that begins and ends in feeling, transforming and interpreting what we feel as we go. So another way to get at the particularity of classical music is by examining its relationship to the emotional power that has generally been celebrated as the most distinctive thing about music in general.

When we say that music "expresses" emotion we don't mean either that it signifies emotion (it's more immediate than that) or that it arouses emotion (it does, but it is scarcely unique in doing so). Music has two specific emotional powers at which it is, if not unrivaled, unsurpassed. First, it renders emotion tangible, giving a sensuous, reproducible form to something otherwise transient and interior. And it does so without sacrificing the force and plasticity of feeling; it does not objectify, but extends subjectivity beyond the boundaries of the nominal self. Second, music detaches emotion from specific motives and circumstances, giving it an independence that is also a form of pleasure, even when the emotions involved are dark or disturbing. And it does so without giving an effect of abstraction; the feelings involved always seem specific, not generic.

How do these expressive qualities reach us, and to what end? According to Ludwig Wittgenstein, who grew up in Vienna in a house visited regularly by the likes of Brahms and Mahler, we understand expression in music the way we understand the expression on a face. Wittgenstein's point was that we grasp the feeling in the hearing of it; we don't decode it or puzzle it out. The analogy captures the point perfectly and feels right besides, but it doesn't quite catch the feeling of musical feeling. To do that, we need to add something. We understand expression in music the way we understand the expression on the face of someone we care about, sympathize with, perhaps even love. This additional element is what bonds us to the music and opens us to its affective powers. The special value we place on song in part comes from this bond, of which the singing voice is the tangible linking thread. As Rousseau remarked, when I hear singing I immediately recognize the presence of another mind, a fellow being, who calls me with an affective tone not necessarily present in speech.

All of these effects, again, belong to music in general, at least in its Western forms. Classical music becomes distinctive by taking its own expressiveness as a beginning and not an end, an opening out and not a closing in. Stretching Wittgenstein's analogy can also be helpful here. The tendency in more vernacular musics is to suggest fulfillment in the fullness of emotion, often a single emotion. The face most popular songs present to us is like the face in a photograph or portrait, or even a snapshot. Like such images, the song may be anything but superficial—a song like the Gershwins' "The Man I Love" is virtually a psychological case study—but it still remains centered on the emotion it explores. In contrast, the tendency in classical music is to seek fulfillment by going beyond emotion without losing or diluting it. The face the classical work presents to us is like the face in a theatrical per-

formance or a film. We can witness its expression changing, often
in subtle and fluid ways, as the feelings involved assume a history,
a context, a past, a future. And because of that we are invited to
grasp what the expression on a face reveals in addition to feeling:
the attitudes, judgments, decisions, and interpretations, the striv-
ings and yieldings, perplexities and insights that form and dissolve amid changing circumstances until some end is reached.
Classical music is drama without stage or actors. Before cinema
was invented, classical music was acoustic cinema.

Of course these distinctions are not hard and fast, and of
course other types of music—I'm thinking of jazz in particular—
like to show changing faces. And of course we would not want to
be without both emotional tendencies. Still and moving images
each give us things the others can't, and so do the types of music
that correspond to them. Yet it's more than a little odd that a culture such as ours, so saturated by the forms of the moving image
combined with music, is so inclined to forget the musical moving
image in favor of musical stills. My point here is simply that if we
want to enjoy and understand the dramas of emotional life, and
the bearing those dramas have on experience and vice versa, then
classical music is an invaluable resource we should not squander.

The modernist art historian Carl Einstein wrote in 1929 that
"[t]he pictorial image is a condensation, a defense against fugitive time and thus against death. One could call it a distillation of
dreams." One could say the same thing about musical "pictures,"
especially popular songs. That may be why songs have such
power of nostalgia. But classical music is rarely at ease with nostalgia; it operates with a different sense of time. To get a sense of
what it offers, of what it is, try a reversal of Einstein's statement:
classical music, the acoustic moving image, is an expansion, an

immersion in fugitive time that is mindful of mortal limits. One could call it an aggregation of dreams.

The classical way of making music with luminous detail and dramatic change is the way I like best. My preference, though, is not very important. Nothing I have to say requires the denigration of other kinds of music; unlike Julian Johnson, I have no interest in making popular music the target of a futile attack. Questions of aesthetic rank have been nothing but harmful to classical music, some of whose devotees have tarred it with unreasonable pretensions to supremacy and universality. My purpose here is not to hold a beauty contest among the musics. It is to explore some of the distinctive things that classical music can do and that can be done with classical music—all things, to my mind, that are very much worth doing. I want to sound this music out so that it can sound out better.

There's no point in denying that classical music demands a bit more effort from the listener than many others: stricter attention, a little technical know-how, a little historical perspective. I sometimes wish that the music had the almost magical capacity of jazz to translate its technical sophistication into immediate musical pleasure. It's also true that classical music can be misused in socially troublesome ways, and I will not shrink from talking about some of these. But from the day that I first accidentally heard a Beethoven overture (someone bought the record by mistake) rocking through the chilly, lifeless suburban "family room" of my early teens with simply unbelievable vehemence, I've been convinced that the music is worth the bother, and more.

It's nearly impossible to compress the reasons why into a formula. I found that out the hard way when working on this book.

People I told about it would ask the obvious question: "Well, why *does* classical music still matter?" Here is what I could glean from my often tongue-tied replies.

It is no good mincing words or hiding behind a false sense of sophistication. This music still matters for the same reason that Greek drama or Renaissance painting or modernist fiction matters: because it made discoveries we are far from done with and that are far from done with us. It has imagined forms of experience that became substantial realities in being thus imagined: forms of being, becoming, sensing, witnessing, remembering, desiring, hoping, suffering, and more.

By making such things audible, classical music enlarges the capacity of all music to attach itself, and us, more closely to whatever we care about. The tradition that tells us to listen to classical works for their own sake alone is an inadvertent betrayal of that care. Music is our premier embodiment of the drive for attachment. It works, it grips or grasps us, almost with the electricity of touch, resonant, perhaps, with the primary experiences of bonding that tie us to each other and the world. Music of all kinds invokes this bonding; classical music dramatizes and reflects on it in the act of invocation.

The power to do this is tangible and exhilarating. It is the power by which we make the world meaningful. Its felt presence is the reason why we keep coming back to the works and styles through which that power runs: coming back to them as sources of pleasure and puzzlement, of self-discovery and self-bafflement. Other music also has things to say to us; there is no doubt about that. But no other music tells us the things that this music does. The Western world is not only the richer for preserving Sophocles' *Antigone* or Beethoven's Ninth Symphony, but different. At one time the difference was available only to a small minority, but technology has long since taken care of that. This music now belongs to anyone who cares to listen. Its fusion of knowledge and power can be demanding, even disturbing. Contrary to the tiresome slogan, classical music does *not* relax you. But it can transfix you, perhaps even transform you. How and why are my subjects in these pages.

CHAPTER TWO

The Fate of Melody
and the Dream of Return

In my beginning is my end.

T. S. ELIOT, *EAST COKER*, FIRST LINE

In my end is my beginning.

T. S. ELIOT, *EAST COKER*, LAST LINE

We can begin by listening closely to some exceptionally beautiful music, immersing ourselves in it, puzzling out what we hear.

Brahms's Clarinet Quintet (1891) begins with a consummation. The solo instrument gleams forth over murmuring strings
in a single harmonious tone. It melts into a lustrous shimmer,
gleams anew, and shimmers again. Then it broadens into a spacious, tranquil melody that slips at the end into the reedy twi-
light of the instrument's lower register. For the first moment or
two the mood is perfectly blissful, to be tinged—just tinged—by
longing or melancholy as the melody expands. What makes this
opening so arresting is not just its sheer sensuous beauty but the

implication that, starting at a point of fulfillment, there is no place to go but down. The very shape of the passage suggests as much. It is as if the formal necessity of expanding the opening moment into a coherent melody entailed the sacrifice of its lyrical self-sufficiency.

This hint is confirmed by everything that follows. The mood of this first movement gradually darkens so that the initial hint of longing becomes charged at the end with deep regret. The clarinet surrenders its melodic self-sufficiency to the strings, which at once introduce qualities of complexity and poignancy that they never surrender. Except in the purely formal repeat of the whole first section, the opening moment of fulfillment is never heard again. It is detached from the rest of the movement to dwell apart in a sphere of its own. Without drama or overt contrast, the passage recedes into the distance while still seeming close by. Throughout the whole movement it hovers tantalizingly just out of reach. The melody comes back, all right, but never intact. It is never quite the same.

Why? Why does Brahms tie this music so closely to the melancholy of transience? Among the many possible answers, one has to do with a deep strain of melancholy widely felt to pervade modern life, another with the melancholy of mortality. Brahms was over sixty, feeling old and creatively exhausted, when he wrote this music. Both he and his century had only a few years left to live. But another reason may go even deeper, reflecting an awareness of both the beauty and the melancholy inherent in music itself. Whether this was Brahms's awareness or only something embodied in the music I can't say. But it points to something that matters deeply about the musical tradition that Brahms inherited and passed down.

My name for that something is old-fashioned; I call it fate. To start getting a sense of it—and getting at its musical sense—we might try shifting from a *why?* question to a *how?* The new question will leave the Clarinet Quintet behind awhile. But the quintet—no surprise in a chapter about returning—will return later, and more than once. You might say it's fated to.

How is it possible to enjoy melody? The question may seem strange, even absurd. No matter what kind of music you favor, the enjoyment of melody is likely to feel utterly natural. On reflection, though, a certain unspoken condition for it appears. To enjoy a melody, we need to be able to hear it more than once. A melody that vanished forever after one hearing would remove itself from the sphere of pleasure to the sphere of regret or indifference. It might not make sense to call such a thing a melody at all. Melody lives by defeating the necessity by which music must vanish in the act of being made. Melody arises as something that lingers and lives as something whose fate is to be restored.

One reason for this is the original identification of melody with the expressive force of the human voice. Historically speaking, instrumental melody derives from vocal melody, and it never wholly forgets its origins, however much it may go its own way. Most of us encounter music first as song, above all as sung by those who care for us as children; many writers have testified to the power of the mother's singing voice, or the singing quality of the mother's voice, in early childhood. Melody is passed from voice to voice, from one singer to another, from one generation to another. And this is not just a circumstantial fact about melody but part of its very concept. Melody sings because it is sung, but to sing at all it must be sung again. It must reach out from the heart of its own necessary transience to be reborn in new conditions, amid new people, in times that have changed. Melody is not just a string of notes: anything but.

Classical music finds its special character in a sustained encounter with this dimension of melody. Most of the music is solidly based on melody, even in the modern period, but to keep the promise that melody makes it must also let melody go. It must learn the fate of melody in order to know itself. The journey that classical melody takes can be perilous, long, and sometimes confusing, but it can bring extraordinary rewards.

As classical music construes its world, and ours, when melody comes back it should come back changed. Its meaning should be different, and so, in most cases, should its form, which both marks new meanings and makes them. Classical melody is left to disappear, even urged to disappear, on behalf of its transformative return. That return is its fate; that fate is its purpose. Classical music wants that fate for melody—the chief expressive resource of Western music—because it wants to take expression as a means rather than an end. It wants to trace the career, the adventures, the chances and mischances of everything that can be expressed. And so classical melody attunes itself to fundamental dramatic scenarios of loss and recovery, desire and destiny, forgetting and remembering, change and recognition.

This quality is also evident elsewhere: in the circular movement through the bridge passage of the classic thirty-two-bar popular song (A A B A) or the cyclical rotation of the equally classic twelve-bar blues (A A B). Such internal bridges are common in the initial melodic statements of classical pieces too. But in classical music the force of departure or dissolution cannot be so neatly contained. The impulse to change often wells up within classical melodies even at the height of their presence. The subsequent event of disappearance and return tends to play out over long spans, sometimes extensive spans. The decision to let this happen creates the imaginary spaces that host it, the internally diverse "movements" one or more of which make up the classical "work."

Classical music constantly puts its claims of beauty, desire, energy, clarity, and so on at risk in the currents of contingency and metamorphosis. This willingness to engage with the passage of time from something like the inside gives the music part of its special character. Classical music allows us to grasp passing time as if it were an object or even a body. Time, which as mutability dissolves the solidity of our loves and beings into abstraction and memory, becomes a source of tangible, persistent pleasure and meaning.

Not that the insistence of loss is forgotten, or forgettable. The living grasp of time only happens for a time. But even where mutability presses hard, its realization as music makes that pressure feel like emotional truth. "Only through time time is conquered," wrote T. S. Eliot in poetry inspired by the late quartets of Beethoven, "music heard so deeply / That it is not heard at all, but you are the music / While the music lasts." While the music lasts: long enough, and yet not long. Thinking of Orpheus, the mythical figure who epitomizes the confrontation of music, time, and loss, Rainer Maria Rilke makes the same realization: "Be as a ringing glass that shatters itself in its ringing." Classical music makes time ring well by wringing it well. Other types of music, composed music less moved by chances and changes or improvised music less bound to melodic substance, can and do conquer time in their own way. But not in just this way.

Or ways: a classical melody can embrace (or resist) its fate in countless ways. Any part of it can be kept, and any part discarded, in the course of its disappearance and return. The rhythm of its coming and going, going and coming, can span a mere instant (the melody is repeated with variation), or occur at intervals, or emerge after long and often tortuous delay (the melody finds itself again, perhaps enhanced, perhaps depleted, after it engages with other melodies or breaks into developing fragments or changes its shape, perhaps again and again). The music we find most memorable is the music that chooses among these possibilities in the most compelling ways. It matters by making the choices matter, finding meaning in them, staking something on them.

The result is something perhaps unique to classical music and at any rate one of its superlative qualities. The works of music that become familiar and beloved assume a distinct personality, in a sense that goes beyond the metaphorical. We take these pieces into our lives, we think and talk about them, the way we do about other minds. We animate them, inspirit them, as we also do with favorite fictional characters and the anthropomorphized things with which we populate our world. We develop an intimacy with them that is as much a kind of companionship as a kind of understanding.

This holds true to a far greater extent of classical music than of other kinds. The classical "work" simulates a personality by dramatizing, through the fate of melody, how that personality came to be. The music tells its own life story. It establishes that story as one to be not just told but retold, revived in new times and new circumstances. But not in new versions—the lifeline for revivals or rerecordings of popular music. No: the repetition has to be exact, the notes changing no more in successive performances than the words of a poem or novel do in successive readings. This principle is flexible in its applications. Even once we allow for the effects of changing performance practice and technology, classical performances, like those readings of texts, retell the music's story without rewriting it. Yet the performances, like the readings, should neither sound quite the same nor mean quite the same. The point has come up before and will again: the performances of a classical work are supposed to replicate the music in detail while differing from each other. This simple fact turns out to have complex ramifications. The one to notice here is that the realization of a classical score depends on the very kind of repetition with difference that it contains as melodic drama. The music lives a form of the drama it enacts.

As with a personality, each new encounter may show a different face, a different side of the same mentality. Large-scale works tend to confront us in full intimate depth, shorter ones in glancing moments of disclosure. This anthropomorphic perception is not a mere illusion or effect but a genuine extension of our sense of personhood—the sense of a singular existence living its allotted time—beyond the boundaries of the person. It is a kind of rational animism that helps us surmount the recurrent disenchantment of the world.

This does not mean that we crudely personify what we hear, but that in hearing we reenact and reinterpret some of the basic terms, the histories and the possibilities, of our lives as persons, and more particularly as modern subjects in the sense developed in chapter 1. Exceptions duly noted, popular musics tend to focus more concretely on the person of the performer, which with classical music (exceptions duly noted) tends to be equaled or exceeded by the "person" of the work. Classical music acts like a spirit in need of a body, which it finds in us when we hearken to it as bodies in need of a spirit. These meetings leave us hungry for more, and for many reasons: because they can seem to touch us at the quick; because they are notoriously hard to describe, which makes them as elusive as they are vivid; and above all because each is by its very nature incomplete no matter how fully achieved it is in the moment. The music demands that we know it again, and better, and in so doing that we know ourselves better, too. We can hear our own fate in the fate of melody, but only if we *make* its fate our own. Like any experience that matters, that resonates, that gets under our skin, this music challenges our power to rise to its occasion. Any difficulty it gives us is not a product of esotericism; it is a product of life.

At this point—speaking of esotericism—it is necessary to face up to the bogey that haunts so many discussions of classical music. What do we do about "form"? What does it have to do with the value of expressive detail and the idea of the fate of melody?

The details of classical music come to matter by the way they participate in the acoustic scenarios through which melody assumes a fate—that is, through which it simultaneously becomes something that can have a fate at all and finds its fate being played out in those very scenarios. The music has a rich vocabulary of qualities with the characteristic of being both immediately perceptible and capable of assuming a rich connotative value, qualities that are simultaneously sensory traits and bearers of meaning. Pace, mobility, shape, texture, color, weight, density, impulse: these terms give some idea of the categories into which the qualities fall, but it is impossible to make an exhaustive list of such categories, much less to list the qualities themselves.

Of course classical music is not unique in this respect; all music, and all art, shares in it. What makes this music distinctive is the sheer abundance, variety, and nuance of these qualities, which generally proliferate in excess of any scenario they help to animate. This proliferation is not simply valued in its own right, though that happens too. As just noted, it is endowed with other meanings and values by being drawn, excess and all, into the unfolding of the expressive or dramatic process. In referring to such processes, I have deliberately avoided the term *form*, though the term is the usual designation for them. The reason is simple enough. I don't want to suggest that classical music matters because its form or structure is complex or interesting. I don't want to suggest that to "appreciate" this music one has to listen for the form. All one has to do is listen. The only requirement is mental and emotional openness, a willingness to hearken.

It is true, though, that describing the music's effects some-times requires references to form, and in this book I will use a minimal, conversational formal vocabulary from time to time. Even so, the emphasis will not be on formal design per se but on the feeling it supports: the sense of something happening, an event, an activity, that goes on within the music. As with musical qualities, no exhaustive list is possible, but some of these activi-ties have historically been preeminent. They include contrast, repetition, variation, development, recapitulation, intensifica-tion, and combination: all easily audible and all as much a part of nonmusical as of musical experience.

These activities are what really matter, not the forms that house them. Traditional forms like sonata, rondo, and the ter-nary cycle (A B A) are important not in themselves but as plat-forms. They are stages on which musical qualities unfold into meaning in the course of a musical action. As such the forms are sources of convenient terms and schemes for describing that unfolding. One doesn't listen *for* the forms, but *through* them. Form arises as a projection of drama; the drama is not a paraphrase tacked onto the form.

What holds true of form also holds for another potentially esoteric, yet expressively vivid, feature of classical music, its harmony. The melodic drama ascribed here to classical music has a familiar harmonic parallel. Tonal music in the classical genres describes an arc away from and back to a primary harmony, the tonic or home key. The route is often circuitous, the departure fascinating, the journey long. But it is important to distinguish between the closed circle of harmony and the open road of melody, between harmonic design and melodic process. The distinction is almost one of ritual versus adventure. Harmony is only an abstraction until it is brought to life in the interplay of melody, texture, and rhythm. Harmonic structure is the stage for the drama of melodic events; it defines the space, sets the scene, creates the atmosphere, but it is subsumed by the action that it houses. This is not to deny its power but to define it. Harmony (tonal and otherwise) gives a concrete audible form to the meaningfulness of melody and its destinies. But it is the melody and the destinies that the meaning befalls, and belongs to.

A simple thought experiment can show the strength of these claims. If you transpose a piece of tonal music from one key to another, the result is a detailed replica of the original. Listeners without perfect pitch will probably not be able to tell the difference between the two or to say which version is the original and which the simulation. But if you keep only the chord progressions of a piece while replacing the original melodies, rhythms, and textures, the result will be a different piece, and probably an incoherent one (unless what you're doing is jazz improvisation, which is another story altogether). Exceptional cases aside, what one hears in a classical piece is not the harmony per se but a melodic and/or rhythmic and/or textural action with a harmonic dimension.

Like drama, classical music both imitates the wishes and chances of living and tries to ritualize them. Like drama, and perhaps even more so, it tries to echo their fundamental rhythms. This process tends to follow one of two general scenarios, which may also combine or overlap or generate mixed or novel types.

The first scenario is cyclical. It identifies the fate of melody with a large symmetrical movement of departure and return. The simplest type (the ternary A B A) consists of a melodic statement, a contrastive middle section, and a return of the opening statement. The music traces a single arc, sometimes with a small addition (a coda) at the close. In more complex types (rondos and rondo-sonatas and strophic variations), the primary melodic statement, the refrain, recurs several times separated by varied episodes. The refrain usually changes en route in response to the episodes, sometimes returning for the last time in its original form, sometimes not.

The other scenario is progressive—the stuff of conflict resolved or not, goals achieved or not, identity formed or not. It relies on no one scheme or design, though it is epitomized by the various realizations of the sonata model, in which conflict, fragmentation, condensation, expansion, and other transformational processes (under the general rubric of development) become both the agents of melodic disappearance and the means of melodic return. The openness to both chances and inevitabilities characteristic of this model links it to the poignant quality that melody can assume both in art and in life when it returns after an absence to memorialize—perhaps to revive, perhaps to mourn, perhaps to render haunting—some experience of great emotional or psychological meaning.

Both these scenarios have already been heard from in the first movement of Brahms's Clarinet Quintet, where the progressive type tries, and fails, to make itself a cyclical whole. Let's treat this music like a melody and hear from it again. What more can we learn from the transformation of its opening moment from a present beauty to a lost ideal, from a melody found in its own unique place to a memory lost in a world of its own?

The passage is presented at the precise moment of its loss. Almost before it can be enjoyed, it becomes the unattainable object of a desire that is the more acute for once having been satisfied. At first the music refuses to recognize this condition of estrangement or to hear in it the sound of a romantic longing very familiar to members of Brahms's generation. The whole first section of the movement (technically speaking, the sonata exposition) is repeated note for note right after it is heard. For the composers who were already Viennese classics for Brahms—the aesthetic trinity of Haydn, Mozart, and Beethoven—this repeat was standard practice, though one that Beethoven had started breaking down in midcareer. By 1891 it was optional, even unusual. Brahms's use of it suggests an attempt to justify hearing the blissful opening passage a second time by appealing to a dated convention: any excuse will do to recapture that moment.

But to be fooled willingly is not quite to be fooled. When the theme comes back, it sounds as if in quotation marks, still lustrous but ever so slightly compromised by the artifice imposed on it, still an object of desire rather than the substance of a fulfillment. Without yet evoking tragedy or even pathos—they come later— the movement has become an elaborate act of mourning for its lost beginning. Every voice in the ensemble, including the clarinet stripped of its best self, must learn to live with this loss.

It is not something they learn easily. The blissful opening almost returns again at the point reserved for its recapitulation, but it breaks down before it can finish, a failed illusion. Later the clarinet tries one last time to recapture it but achieves only frustration. The result is a travesty, a hysterical outburst on the theme followed by its dissolution, with which the movement ends. This music understands the fate of melody, and even wins a considerable measure of beauty and strength from it—the very thing it is supposed to do. But it is not satisfied, and it will not pretend to be.

Classical music, popular music, and jazz might all be said to meet on the ground of melody. They borrow from each other shamelessly, all knowing a good thing when they hear it. But they don't treat their melodies in the same way, and the distinct value of each depends on the treatment. For simplicity's sake, let's just settle on a contrast—but not a contest—between classical and popular types, recognizing quite well that each term loosely lumps together a multitude of styles. The types are ideals, to which by no means all melodies of either type correspond. And we would be the poorer for lacking either; there is clearly no need to choose between them. But if we want our musical experience to mirror the dynamism of experience and our struggle to make sense of it, the risks and rewards of change and transformation, the sense of what it means to have a destiny, then classical melody is an invaluable resource.

Most popular melodies are all of a piece, self-contained wholes sustaining or deepening a single mood. They are meant mainly to be repeated in different voices, styles, textures, and levels of intensity, and they may be repeated at will. Their availability is part of the pleasure they offer. Their treatment may be simple or complex, direct or allusive, compact or expansive; their single focus is a metier, not a constraint. Just think of the range of what is now often called the American songbook, from, say, the disarming directness of Irving Berlin to the wavering balance of irony and sentiment in Cole Porter to the fearless emotional probing of Ray Charles.

Most classical melodies are either less than a whole or less wholly self-contained. Those that are less than a whole consist of single phrases or subphrases (motives, figures, thematic ideas), expressive fragments from which a whole must somehow be made, or almost made, or never quite made. These little phrases may be quite haunting and compelling in their inability to be settled. Those melodies that do present themselves as wholes are full and rounded, with phrases that interlock and balance each other. But most of these melodies are nonetheless divided against themselves, marked by internal difference, by contrast or conflict, sometimes sharp, sometimes subtle. Sometimes this self-division is the very principle that shapes the melody; the phrases that compose the melodic whole harbor different tendencies, different feelings, different attitudes. Sometimes the division involves a contrastive utterance framed by two rounded statements of a more uniform melody, the second of which is usually less stable than the first. The larger musical whole comes into being as the differences internal to melody play themselves out through time. Few classical melodies are allowed to go for long without meeting a partner or a rival, a figure that answers or questions, a counterpart or contrary.

The two types of classical melody are constantly in dialogue with each other, approaching or avoiding one another, fostering or checking each other, commenting, enhancing, subverting, inciting. With both types (ideal types, of course, that often intermix, just as the cyclical and progressive scenarios do), classical melody embodies an impulse to significant change. The fate of melody is always a meaningful process. The fragmentary melodies are committed by their very nature to the process that will vindicate and clarify them, and they cannot be pried apart from that process. They cannot be repeated without being transformed. The rounded melodies are paradoxically full in themselves yet not fulfilled until they have played out the changes, the date with time and chance, embedded in their very fullness. We want to hear such melodies again, not just because they are beautiful or moving, but because they embody a promise that can only be kept in the fullness of time. Their repetition is not something to be assumed (the case for popular melody); it is something to be accomplished.

When classical melodies are not given over to change, the exception is not taken for granted but marked, noted, problematized, interpreted. Rounded forms that either lack internal difference or decline to play it out through time are rarities, special cases that bear a special value. These closed melodies tend to present themselves as precious objects, numinous things that can somehow be possessed by the listener, to whom they make a kind of gift, perhaps of insight, perhaps of illusion, or from whom they demand a special recognition, perhaps ecstatic, perhaps tragic. They tend to stand apart from the dialogue of melodic types that surrounds them. They inhabit a world of their own that disrupts or delays, inspires or guides, the world of change and conflict on which they impinge. The opening of the Brahms Clarinet Quintet is arresting in part because it takes this kind of melody as a premise, without rationalization or apology.

The history of these possibilities begins in the mid-eighteenth century with the shift from open Baroque melody, designed for "spinning out," to classical periodic (rounded, symmetrical) melody. Although the shift isn't absolute—Bach and others sometimes write rounded melodies, and motivic writing similar to spinning out is basic to the classical vocabulary—the stylistic reorientation is significant, even a watershed.

The difference in melody corresponds, as always, to a shift of subjectivity, a change in the climate of feeling. In this case it establishes a broad range of dramatic possibilities. Open melody regards the subject, the person who feels and knows, primarily as an unfinished participant in a continuous process—be it spiritual, social, educative, or the like. Rounded melody subsumes the open type without simply abolishing it. A product of the European Enlightenment, rounded melody regards the subject primarily as an individual, a self-enclosed being who must be drawn into relationship with other persons and conditions, even when the latter are the very basis of the subject's identity. Such different subjects hear, make, and perform music in their own distinctive and historically vibrant ways. Classical music is, so to speak, their laboratory and their playing field. And the question of just how rounded melody enters the field of change—through breakdown, seduction, desire, compulsion, self-surrender, impulse, concession, obliviousness, forethought, and so on and so forth; there is no normative reason—establishes one of classical music's primary dimensions of musical meaning.

The question forms the dramatic pivot in the first movement of Tchaikovsky's Sixth Symphony, the "Pathetique" (1893; the subtitle refers to passion rather than pathos, though by its close the symphony has done away with the difference). The second section of this movement is a large self-contained whole in which one closed lyrical theme encloses another. The strings take up the lush outer melody, solo woodwinds the more intimate, more vulnerable inner one; a sensuous envelope folds around a sensitive core. This melodic bubble famously bursts when a brutal outburst from the full orchestra—a short, vicious swipe of sound— shatters the stillness that has gathered around the outer melody's close. Sheer turmoil follows, and lots of it. When the lyrical section recapitulates after the violence is spent, the inner theme does not return, as if it were no longer possible to voice it. The fate of this sensitive melody was to be extinguished. Nor does the outer theme return intact. Lacking its partner, it can return only once, its texture subtly frayed by changes in orchestration. After that it fades into an epilogue that ends the movement.

Whatever the outer melody hoped to offer survives only in a semiempty form, still courting belief but unable to reward it. And if one does believe it, does one also have to believe the things that come after that downcast ending? The limping bonhomie of the second movement? The third movement's iron-fisted call to order, duty, and forced ardor, climaxing with *all-together-now!* brutality? The long dying-away of a lamenting theme to a low groan on bassoons and lower strings that is the sole substance of the finale?

The questions, like the musical moments, go together. What vanishes at the end of the first movement is the inner and inward-looking melody sung by solo voices in dialogue, not the communal anthem of the string choir. The fate of the solo or solitary voice matters greatly in this symphony, which embodies it in an instrument rarely granted much limelight, the lowly bassoon. (The bassoon voice sounds on two instruments when acoustically necessary, but it is always single.) In the original lyric passage, the solo flute, solo clarinet, and choir of upper winds successively draw the bassoon into the light to share the inner melody. Afterwards, the winding-down of the outer melody ends with the unaccompanied bassoon holding the note that the orchestra's fist shatters. The dialogues fulfill the longing revealed in the first moments of the symphony, in which the bassoon voice alone makes articulate the deep darkness of the lower strings. The shattering prefigures the loss of that articulateness in the symphony's last moments when the bassoon, together with the work as a whole, subsides into that same darkness. The German social philosopher Walter Benjamin once wrote that to have a fate is to be found guilty regardless of one's actions. The fate of the bassoon in this symphony is to suffer the guilt of seeking a voice when the privilege of voice is denied one. But if the fate is dark, the voice is irrevocable. The bassoon pays. But it sings.

Brahms, whose music Tchaikovsky hated, or so he said, gives a solitary rounded melody a more congenial treatment—a fate without fatality or fatalism—in the slow movement of his Violin Concerto (1878). The movement begins by giving its wistful main melody, not to the soloist, but to the solo oboe, which spins it out caressingly at length, almost as if no violin were waiting in the wings. This theme is the source of the violin's own abundant melody, but only as an absence that haunts everything the violin does, even when it does more than the melody could dream of. The violin can vary or embellish the oboe's melody or elaborate on fragments of it; it can engage in ornamentation or counter-melody when the oboe returns to sing again (but never again at full length; not even the oboe can do that); the only thing the violin can't do with this melody is play it. The resemblance to the situation of the Clarinet Quintet is clear. The soloist inherits the melody as a beatific ideal but can never quite take full possession of it. Its dispossession leads to flights of great serenity and beauty, but it is still dispossession.

In relation to the violin, the oboe's melody is always in the distance. Approaching it is like trying to copy a Platonic form: you can't get it exactly right no matter what you do, so you must make do with what you can get. The theme voices a blissful contentment that is not unattainable, but never attainable in the way one has imagined. A longing for the unattainable might actually have been easier to cope with. As things are, whatever the violin does, no matter how exquisite, something is always left out. The music constantly circles around a gap that can be filled only with longing and nostalgia.

Yet nothing forced Brahms to write the oboe passage; no one commanded him to deny the melody to the violin. Why did he do it? Again, the question resembles the one raised by the Clarinet Quintet, and the answer—one likely answer—involves a bit more of the historical picture. The outcome is more hopeful than one might at first expect.

By insisting on an imperfect yet unflawed bliss, Brahms reflects the widespread belief of his era that the conditions of modern life had diminished the power, one might almost say the art, of feeling. Passion and desire were no longer what they were even one or two generations before. And they had not declined gradually but suffered a precipitous falling off. This belief, this experience, received a memorable expression from Matthew Arnold in his poem "Memorial Verses," which symbolizes the dark historical turn by the death of a culture hero, in this case William Wordsworth:

> Time may restore us in his course
> Goethe's sage mind and Byron's force;
> But where will Europe's latter hour
> Again find Wordsworth's healing power?
> Others will teach us how to dare,
> And against fear our breast to steel;
> Others will strengthen us to bear—
> But who, ah! who, will make us feel?

Had Arnold been a musician, he would almost certainly have named Beethoven. The point would have been the same. The legacy of such giants exhausts its own gifts. Modern life can honor but not reproduce them. For Brahms to write the oboe passage was in part an expression of this insight and also—since the movement is beautiful and unclouded—an effort to show by what follows that the loss is not absolute. One can almost come to forget it, or at least edge it to a far corner of the mind. But this also makes the expressive act an ethical one. Not to write the passage would have been to lie.

And the truth is rewarded. Heard at a remove, the theme on the oboe assumes a pastoral charm, an archaic enchantment often associated with the instrument's reedy plaintiveness. The soloist can emulate this quality if not wholly possess it; unlike the Clarinet Quintet, the Violin Concerto does not foreclose the fate of melody. Instead, the concerto's shift from the distanced voice of the oboe to the here-and-now voice of the soloist opens the pathos of distance for enjoyment. It makes possible the discovery of a nostalgia without tears, a strange but satisfying blend of longing, melancholy, and pleasure.

Melody in the music we have just been examining assumes the value of a treasured, numinous object. The music at large explores the inevitable loss of such an object and the striving to regain it. The expressive arc in pieces like this depends on the question of whether melodic flux, the necessity of melody to disappear in favor of other sounds, is to be resisted or embraced. Do we try to make at least one melody something closed, possessed, relatively immutable until something disturbs it? Or do we open ourselves unreservedly to the flux, change, and transformation into which any melody must inevitably lapse?

Another expressive arc, equally important, depends on whether the return of melody, together with the musical world built up around it, including secondary melodies, occurs as a repetition or as a recapitulation. Here once again we encounter a question of form, not as a matter primarily of technique, but as a vehicle of value and significant experience, and with nothing arcane about it. Repetition is literal, or nearly so. Its effect is one of conservation, preservation, observance, equilibrium; its model is the symmetry of the A B A pattern. Recapitulation is transformational. Its effect is one of progression, enrichment, consequence, intensification, or at times their contraries, effects of collapse or decline. It moves along a spiral, not in a circle.

The initial effect of the circular pattern is to give a sense of roundness and completeness to a varied whole, with the middle section normally providing the contrast. Obvious meanings, both social and psychological, attach to proceeding this way. Many circular pieces, for example, involve the disciplining or unleashing of an energy that is both bodily and social. Pieces based on dance forms like the minuet and waltz focus on controlled energy; pieces of more festive or mischievous character—scherzos—focus on energy let loose. Just what it means to enjoy these energies depends on how their disappearance and return plays out, and thus on how the sections that express them differ from the middle section.

Contrast here is not just an aesthetic concern. The meaning of what happens emerges only in the movement of return through the difference of the middle. The middle section represents a step outside the firm borders set by the primary section, a movement beyond what is known or believed, regulated or possessed. The two sections are often divided by no more than a little pause, without transition, but this minuscule divider is actually a threshold or corridor that can be dangerous to cross. A great deal may depend on it, brief and often inaudible though it may be. The danger particularly haunts the way back, which may try to ward it off with a transition to ease the return. The crossing can also be trouble free, as many examples indicate. But the possibility of risk never disappears.

The risks themselves come in many guises. The middle sections of socially oriented pieces (the dances and scherzos) may harbor energies that make their outer sections seem stolid or dreams that make them seem crude. Reflective, inward-looking pieces (certain slow movements or Romantic piano pieces) may pass through psychological or emotional extremes from which there is really no return, conditions that no amount of reflection can contain.

In other cases it is the middle section that may go awry. It may fail to live up to the promises of the outer sections, or it may squander their emotional or social energy. Either way, whether its contrast is too weak or too strong, the middle section is the potential source of trouble. The more it goes its own way, the more it may undermine its foreordained appointment with the return of the primary section. The conclusion of the middle section forms a symbolic threshold similar to the one classically located by the anthropologist Mary Douglas between different social territories. "All margins," she notes, "are dangerous. If they are pulled this way or that the shape of fundamental experience is altered. Any structure of ideas is vulnerable at its margins." This vulnerability becomes particularly acute when the human body is involved, pulled this way or that by forces of restraint and release, order and impulse. The expressive body language of many singers and instrumental soloists (and some conductors) serves to identify musical performance as this sort of threshold experience. Music, rich in bodily qualities of its own, makes the experience part of itself with each transition between different expressive territories. Its essays in circular repetition depend on the power of symmetry to manage the powers and dangers attendant on every crossing of a threshold.

But the mix of power and danger is unstable. Over time, the power of melodic return to assimilate contrast declines; symmetry loses its magic. This happens with increasing frequency across the nineteenth century, by the end of which the circular return has lost most of its credibility. Where it appears, the circular close is a kind of credo. And like most credos, it becomes more anxious and unsteady, more in need of supplements to shore it up, as the skeptical mentality of modernity looms ever larger.

What replaces the broken circle is the dialectical spiral. At its simplest, this is a return that changes in response to the middle section. The change reinterprets what has preceded it, as if the music itself had been listening. Mozart suggests the need for such a change in the slow movement of his Piano Concerto in D Minor, composed in 1785. But he does not satisfy the need he uncovers. Perhaps the time was not yet right; the problem itself was in its infancy. Simply exposing it was both prescient and brave. The music contains a famous disruption, but what is most remarkable about it is its willingness to let the disruption pose a question that Mozart's musical language has no way to answer.

The first movement of this concerto is one of the most agitated, dark, and conflicted pieces of the eighteenth century. It ends without resolution, subsiding rather than concluding. The slow movement, identified as a "Romance" *(Romanze)*, at first seems to occupy a different world. Its refrain is simple, elegant, placid, even a bit insipid. It places its trust in poise, restraint, the cultivated regulation of feeling; it is reluctant to accept that its melody has any fate other than sheer repetition. The music is lulling, an example of practiced forgetfulness. It also forms a circular pattern in its own right, enfolding a more warmly colored lyrical interlude in its pastel embrace. The feeling in the interlude is heightened, even touched by yearning and unrest, but it is not, it is anything but, extravagant. It is authentic precisely in shunning extravagance.

Then the turbulence of the earlier movement comes crashing back. The middle section of the Romanze is also an interlude, a disruptive minor-key interlude crisscrossed by sharp exclamations, wailing woodwind phrases, and fast-moving sweeps across the keyboard, all brusquely dismissing the romance as so much marzipan. More pressing, almost literally so, is the impression of continuous agitation, a revelation of psychological urgency or blind mechanism beating against the bounds of civilized restraint. Like the first movement, this interlude dies down for reasons of its own. But it accepts no limits on its passions.

The return of the refrain after this—unchanged except for a few embellishments and leading into a beatific epilogue—is disquieting. It disquiets not just because the contrast is extreme, and not just because the refrain acts as if nothing important has happened. It disquiets because the larger circle of the movement as a whole contradicts the smaller circle earlier traced by the refrain. The refrain and the middle section live by different values. How can the same principle that governs the refrain's measured dreaminess also govern the very forces that leave the dream in tatters?

The fact that Mozart follows the principle in the end does not mean it remains intact. The middle section articulates a rift between feeling and logic, heart and head, sincerity and civility, expression and symbol, that was one of the chief preoccupations of the eighteenth century and one of its chief legacies. The piano's outburst expresses a depth of passion that may not be containable by any symbolic means. There may just be no way to rationalize what has been felt, and may be felt again. The refrain, on its last return, asks us to forget this, too. But there is no guarantee that we will or even that we want to.

Two generations later, and the guarantee is all on the other side. The slow movement of Schubert's Piano Sonata in A, composed in 1828, transfers Mozart's concern with sincerity versus civility to a preoccupation with dark self-knowledge. Schubert, we're told, had a temper. Asked once what would happen if he lost it, he replied through gritted teeth that it had never happened—*yet*. The music gives a different answer.

The melody of Schubert's refrain is less effusive than Mozart's, but perhaps for that reason it is even more vulnerable. Its tone is one of Romantic melancholy, a pleasing sadness that is not as different from Mozart's Arcadian placidity as we might suppose. Both feelings are idealized; a sense of distance imbues them both. But differences grow. Schubert's central outburst makes Mozart's seem almost reasonable. It starts less aggressively but grows steadily wilder and more extravagant, feeding on itself like an improvisation out of control, its climax crazed to the point of hysteria, a gypsy imitation gone bad, very bad. The violence eventually collapses into a musical rubble, a series of little fragments that lasts palpably too long. For a moment or two the sounds almost stop being music.

The job of picking up the pieces falls to the piquant initial theme—but these pieces have sharp edges. When the theme returns it comes beset by haltings and stabbings, pulsations from above and nervous wriggles from below that disturb the theme's mood and the credibility of its unity with itself. The additions persist for a long time before receding. They replicate the sensations with which Schubert's era identified nervous disorder, a piercing throb and a persistent shudder. The Romantic melancholy of the theme has become a symptom.

Yet this continued disruption solves the problem raised but left hanging by Mozart's Romanze. The returning theme can absorb, if not wholly integrate, the shock of the central outburst. It can acknowledge, if not wholly rationalize, the outburst's force. By recapitulating, not just repeating, the initial melody opens itself up to the meanings of the events it precipitates and to unsuspected dimensions of its own meaning. It becomes a form of remembering, not of forgetting, even if what is remembered is unaccountable.

The difference between Mozart and Schubert is the difference between a demand for recognition that feeling is not always bounded by reason and a plunge into a traumatic irrationality that defies recognition in principle. Both composers ask how music can both register the experience of pain, disorientation, shock, even frenzy, and assimilate the knowledge of such things to an intact self or community. Mozart's answer is implicit and perhaps evasive. "By upholding a transparent fiction of wholeness," he says—but perhaps halfheartedly. (The halfheartedness is what we should thank him for. As for the beauty of the epilogue, he just can't help himself.) Schubert, not satisfied with that, is explicit and unshrinking. "By the music's disfiguring itself," he says— adding, however, that such disfigurement has its own strange sort of beauty.

The Brahms Clarinet Quintet understands the problem of repetition and recapitulation all too well. We've already seen that its first movement is allowed to founder because it can have the second but not the first. Now we need to return to the fate of melody in this music one last time.

When the first movement ends, its dilemma of longing and mourning for lost bliss does not end with it. By slow and difficult steps, that dilemma seeks a resolution over the course of what remains. In the middle section of the slow movement, another failed attempt to recall the blissful moment precipitates a wild "gypsy" lament by the clarinet, a keening evocative of something balladlike, archaic and unappeasable. The spirit is close to that of Schubert's outburst in the A-Major Piano Sonata, though Brahms, unlike Schubert, fights shy of the bizarre and the grotesque; he wants to forestall the kind of disfigurement that Schubert admits, regardless of the depth of unreasoning anger and longing. An unappeasable spirit also haunts the finale, which is a set of variations on an unstated theme. Before very long, it becomes clear that the theme is the opening of the first movement, the music of lost bliss. The finale is in search of it, hoping against hope to end the quintet with its recovery: "In my end is my beginning."

If nothing else, the hope is to amend the sense of loss, even if it cannot be remedied, by saying an appropriate farewell. So the music goes systematically rummaging around in memory or fantasy (unable, really, to tell them apart) until it finds what it wants, which may or may not be what it has so long sought. The bliss is this music's secret, a secret kept even from the music itself so that in the end it can be discovered, blurted out, confessed. Yet when it appears at last the blissful melody smothers the desire it rewards. It collapses one last time—really the last, this time—into a gloomy, dark-toned B-minor close on the strings. The long search has only reconfirmed the transformation of a once-present happiness into an eternally lost object of desire. What the quintet learns from that transformation is the hard necessity of resigning oneself to it.

This necessity is both historical and, for lack a better word, metaphysical. The music stands as a meditation on what music can and can't give us. It suggests that we, too, need to learn a certain resignation, that we need to listen with resignation as well as with pleasure. Music, it says, cannot offer to give what life refuses us. That we may want it to nonetheless, and may never stop wanting it to, is also one of the truths that the quintet exposes.

Yet it is not the whole truth, and we can appreciate the hard-won integrity required to entertain it without necessarily embracing it as our own. The quintet offers us the choice. It lays a great deal of emphasis, perhaps too much, on loss and resignation amid a rich, gleaming beauty that it never for a moment ceases to create. Do we really have to burden our pleasure with *this* much sadness?

Brahms himself suggests otherwise in his Violin Concerto, admittedly an earlier work. So, too, does Tchaikovsky in his Piano Concerto no. 1 in B♭ Minor, one of the most widely played of all classical works, premiered in 1876, just two years before the Brahms. Like Brahms's Clarinet Quintet, Tchaikovsky's concerto begins at a peak of magnificence that it never regains; regaining it is assumed to be impossible. But unlike Brahms Tchaikovsky makes no attempt to regain it. He even sets it at a distance, in a key not the concerto's own, a harmonic place apart. The introduction forms a self-enclosed circular pattern with a quasi-improvisatory solo flight for a middle section. The departure from this rounded whole comes gradually. The opening melody crumbles away; in its wake, the piano goes off in search of a new theme, which simply materializes in the course of another quasi-improvisatory passage. The concerto proper takes place in the space of possibility opened by this departure. Inevitably, there is plenty of romantic longing there. But the concerto does not suffer with that longing; it seems to revel in it. The absence of the original inspiration is neither a loss nor, like the oboe theme in Brahms's Violin Concerto, a lack, even a fertile lack.

The concerto treats the disappearance of its sublime point of origin as a premise, not a fatality. Tchaikovsky, supposedly the more emotional composer, is here the more restrained.

If Brahms increasingly felt that we should, or that *he* should, assume a pervasive sense of loss or lack as normal, the reason may lie less in the human condition at large than in the conditions of life in the world that increasingly confronted him. It was a world becoming more modern every day. Like Paris before it, Vienna had been engaged for decades in an aggressive program of urban development, both commercial and residential. In 1894 the city began construction of its municipal railway system, which by the time it was done in 1904 would put up more than thirty stations as well as a plethora of viaducts, tunnels, and bridges. The chief architect, Otto Wagner, wrote in 1895 that "THE ONLY POSSIBLE POINT OF DEPARTURE FOR OUR ARTISTIC CREATION IS MODERN LIFE. . . . [We must] do justice to the colossal technical and scientific achievements as well as to the fundamentally practical character of modern mankind." By the time Brahms died in 1897, the modernizing process was as irresistible as a speeding train.

Yet amid all the commercial and civic vigor, the sense of modernity at the fin de siècle was often deeply melancholy. Modern technology seemed to sully the pristine authenticity of experience. Modern social organization eroded the sense of true community, the feeling of belonging to a homogenous organic society (something that in Brahms's world, but not to Brahms, too often meant a society without Jews). Modern nervousness, an epidemic of physical and nervous malaise—the new term was *neurosis*—seemed to be breaking out as one of the leading discontents of modern civilization. The feeling that life was at best a hopeless search for its own earlier radiance became widespread.

In this climate of feeling, the elder Brahms slipped easily into the role of an "autumnal" figure, and Brahms in general came to embody the prevailing nostalgia, the "transcendental homelessness," that would consolidate the experience of modernity as one of essential alienation. Nietzsche, the most music-loving of philosophers but one rarely sympathetic to Brahms, captures this idea while resisting his own involvement with it: "[Brahms's] is the melancholy of incapacity. . . . [W]hat [is] specifically his is *yearning*. This is felt by all who are full of yearning and dissatisfaction of any kind. He is too little a person, too little a center. . . . Brahms is touching as long as he is secretly enraptured or mourns for himself—in this he is 'modern.'"

Like Brahms's Clarinet Quintet, and his earlier Third Symphony, many classical pieces of the late nineteenth and early twentieth century conclude after a circular movement. They repeat, recall, or enlarge on an earlier moment to reach the end, as if by doing so they can achieve—symbolically, at least—the return to social and emotional integration that Brahms treats so skeptically.

As Brahms shows, what matters is not simply that the melody returns but how it returns and what has become of it. The significance of a cyclical return can range from the most cosmic to the most worldly. Mahler's Second Symphony of 1894, subtitled "Resurrection," begins with a despairing funeral march and ends with a beatific celebration in which solo and choral voices join the orchestra to declare their faith in deliverance from death—literally so, perhaps, but figuratively even more. The music draws on apocalyptic imagery to imagine the overcoming of spiritual destitution. The first movement, the march, includes a tranquil ascending theme that dispenses a spirit of consolation if not of transcendence. Five movements later, transcendence comes in the shape of the same theme but with different scoring, a new contour, and a new key: the form, we're asked to hear, of the theme's immortality. This is the form in which it may be sung. Mahler added some lines to his preexisting text suggesting that the effect of transcendence is less something the music expresses than something it does, something it accomplishes: "With wings I have won for myself / Will I soar aloft in striving love / To the light."

Olivier Messiaen would never claim so much; a man of intense religious faith, he combines musical ambitiousness with spiritual humility. His *Quartet for the End of Time* of 1940, an intimate chamber work composed in a Nazi prison camp, looks beyond the dismay of the present to a transfigured future. It conceives the end of time as neither terrifying nor jubilant but as possessed by a spirit of ever-increasing serenity in the face of terror and jubilation.

The work is in eight movements, corresponding to the seven days of Creation plus one. The second and seventh of these deal with the angel of the Apocalypse, a magnificent figure garlanded by rainbows. In the second movement, identified as an instrumental vocalise, the ensemble (clarinet, violin, cello, and piano) "speaks" for the angel in contrasting voices. Short fast-moving passages of violent majesty frame a broad, slow, serene contemplation for violin and cello backed by shimmering piano chords. In the seventh movement, addressed as a "cluster of rainbows" *to* the angel, the contemplation returns but the framing violence is gone. The spirit echoes the angel's gentleness, not his sternness. The cello marks the reversal by preceding the entrance of the violin, reversing the order of the earlier passage and changing its initial mood from tentative to secure. The fate of melody here is to close a circle within the linear progress of the work as a whole. That leaves the eighth movement to reside in perfect tranquility beyond the circuit of human time.

A similar return grounds a sense of civic rather than religious deliverance in Leos Janacek's 1926 *Sinfonietta*. The music is a celebratory tour of the Czech composer's hometown of Brno in a newly won state of political independence. It culminates in an enriched return of the whole first movement embedded in the last. The work ends when the returning movement extends beyond its original close to reach what seems a predestined peak of grandeur.

This first movement is a vibrant series of three closely related fanfares for an outdoorsy multitude of trumpets (nine of them just for the melody) backed by tubas and timpani. The fanfares are splashes of primary color, as short and simple as they are exuberant. The trumpets proclaim the opening flourish over and over, then switch to the next to do the same, then do the same with the third; the music is a festive juggernaut. This technique of building a movement from a string of short episodes is typical of Janacek, and the remainder of the piece mostly does just that, often juxtaposing episodes of startlingly different character. The first movement stands apart not only for its jubilance but also for its single-mindedness. This music is going somewhere; to get there it has to be recapitulated; and it is the only music in the *Sinfonietta* that will be.

But should we hear this recapitulation as an end or a beginning? The chronological beginning, the original first movement, breaks off abruptly, juxtaposed with something radically different.

When it eventually returns, the movement does more than just begin again; it begins for the first time as a fully meaningful event. The intervening episodes, the sounds drawn from the sites that map the town, supply the movement with the one thing it lacked before: the history whose outcome its fanfares proclaim. We can hear this enrichment in the strings and winds that now add their colors to the radiance of the brass. We might have heard it coming in traces of fanfare seeded in the second and third movements. The piece begins with the end, or almost the end, then shows us how we got there. By doing so it reveals the end as the true beginning, a social and communal beginning that is celebrated, paradoxically, by the subsequent sounds of musical closure. It is this public ratification, this faith in organic society, that allows the logic here to be exactly the opposite of that in the Brahms Quintet but the secular parallel to that of the Messiaen Quartet. The concluding return of the origin is not a farewell but a greeting, not the record of a loss but the presence of a transfiguration.

George Gershwin's *An American in Paris* also constructs an image of an ideal city, but in terms far more racy and urbane than Janacek's, which it follows by just two years. The virtue of civic life has become the pleasure of café society. Tradition yields to the pulse of traffic, symbolizing modern mobility and symbolized by four French taxi horns that Gershwin famously acquired and wrote into his score.

Beneath the apparent flippancy, however, something is genuinely at stake. The piece culminates with a reprise of its central episode, a luscious lyrical blues. At first a majestic outburst by the full orchestra, the reprise ebbs away into a delicate series of instrumental solos, wistful and fleeting. This transformation is richly ambivalent. It subsumes the prevailing high spirits under the banner of romance but with an undertone of dissatisfied reflection. It simultaneously sums up the freewheeling, hedonistic spirit of the Jazz Age and summons it up as something already in retreat. The progressive spirit of modernity turns out to contain its own nostalgia, not so far removed from the spirit of Brahms as one might think. The boisterous, even raucous, finish that follows can pooh-pooh this impression but not make it disappear. Literally not: a fragment of the blues melody actually ends the piece a few seconds after the full melody gets a complete, unexpected, and achingly nostalgic extra reprise.

Examples could be multiplied endlessly. So rooted, so culturally fraught, is the principle of melodic return that its own return is virtually irrepressible. It seems like the force of nature itself, of a piece with traditional conceptions of cyclical time. By the same token, forgoing melodic return, sometimes by forgoing melody altogether, readily presents itself as a way of breaking with tradition. For that reason it became one of the chief traits of aggressive modernism in the twentieth century.

Modernism in one of its definitions is a principled hostility to all traditions, including the traditions of personhood. To break the mold of melody is to break the mold of a false or impoverished identity. We all know the feeling of being beset by a melody we find suspect, a melody that somehow degrades us. For some composers, the burdens of twentieth-century life rendered all melody suspect. Some would forswear it ascetically in the service of some supposedly higher ideal, including the continuous, nonrepeating transformation of what would otherwise be the melodic line. Others would ask the absence of melody, the suspension of its articulateness, to uphold an encounter with music as a purely sensory or rhythmic phenomenon. Some modernist music seeks the unmixed pleasure of color and texture; some aims at immersion in a directionless mass of sound, free of ulterior motives. These are rich possibilities that I can do no more than acknowledge here. But however rich they are, they remain a subplot. The fate of melody and the dream of return are stubborn forces, and strong. The kinds of identity they invoke are widely believed in and widely desired. Even in the modernist century, melodic drama more than held its own. It remains the heart of the matter, and the heart of what matters, in classical music.

CHAPTER THREE

Score and Performance, Performance and Film

Classical Music as Liberating Energy

The fate of melody is the first great differential feature of classical music. The melody in this music does not express its fate but meets it, has it, finds it. Grasping the fate of melody, in all its luminous detail, is not something to do while listening to classical music—it *is* listening to classical music. The fate of melody is what the composer composes; it is what the score inscribes.

Mention of the score brings us to the second great differential, the eternal dialogue of score and performance. The fate of melody is what the performance performs as well as what the composer composes. That fate is something the performers know through their playing—they follow the score, even memorize it—but it is also more than that. It is something they *get* to know through their playing. The performance of a score makes the fate of melody an event to be discovered and explored, not just to be observed, and as the performers get to know it so, too, do their listeners. What they find out may be altered or affected by both the particular qualities of the performance and the real or fictional circumstances in which the music is heard. This process can have profound repercussions. It not just a peculiarity of classical music but another key to why classical music still matters.

One of the defining experiences of my musical life was my first encounter with Beethoven's String Quartet no. 12 in E^b, op. 127, performed live by the Juilliard String Quartet. I was in college at the time; I knew something about "late Beethoven" and the magic and elevation associated with the phrase, but I did not yet know this piece. The opening bars that night touched me with the force of a revelation. The whole quartet made an overwhelming impression that has only deepened over the years, but those opening bars were incomparable. They begin with deep, full, rich chords, filling up the resonant spaces above open fifths in the cello and viola with pure consonance, making a sound at once consoling and almost intimidating in its power and majesty. They continue, with a kind of blissful shudder on solo violin, into a melodic passage entwining all four voices with extraordinary tenderness and sweetness.

The combination plays out over the whole quartet, and it was just what I needed that night. I had come to the concert troubled in mind, lonely, more than a little angry and defensive, beset by unresolved difficulties in romance and friendship. I left feeling reconciled with the prospects of both success and failure in resolving my problems, and I still carry with me the memory of walking slowly across a broad expanse of fresh green lawn (it was early spring) lit by a providentially full moon that seemed to do for the landscape what the music had done for me. What I had heard, in those opening bars especially, was the ability of strong, almost violent depth of feeling to change in a moment to the most rapturous tenderness. The contrast between the two was not a gulf but a span across which one could freely move.

I heard all this in the music; I still do. But in later years, after hearing the same music often, performed by many other groups, I came to realize that I heard these things not in the music alone but in that single and singular performance of it—something I just happened to need urgently, though I did not know that until the music sounded. The Juilliard bit into those opening chords with a ferocity barely contained by the consonant harmonies; . they caressed the melody afterwards with a serenity and a confidence that was almost a fifth voice in the ensemble. The music affected me as deeply as it did, not as an abstract work, but as something that came alive for me just one particular night in an experience that could be revisited but never repeated.

So what touched me more, the music or the performance? At the risk of posing the question with another one invoked too often, how would I form the musical answer to Yeats's famous version: "O body swayed to music, O brightening glance, / How shall we tell the dancer from the dance"?

The question is particularly pointed when asked of classical music. As we've noted before, this music maps its own performance with unusual fullness. Unlike performers in popular traditions, classical performers cannot partly recompose the music in the act of playing it. Some limited exceptions aside, they cannot vary the music, embellish it freely, change its melodic shape, abridge it, expand it, change its tempo or instrumentation or harmony. They have to play the notes in the score. Classical music is an art of revisitation or reanimation; it brings back elapsed works in the same way that those works, within themselves, bring back elapsed melodies.

This state of affairs has far-reaching consequences. The possibility of repeatedly performing the same score in different ways and under different circumstances approximates the feeling of living in time. It endows the music with a lifelike sense, an animate aura, almost a sentience. This is one of the sources of a quality we met with in the preceding chapter. As long as we want to keep rehearing it, the classical work takes on a virtual life similar to that of a fictional character whose slightly uncanny reality is in no way compromised by mere lack of existence. The work of music, though it has no physical form, assumes a tangible personality, an individual identity with which a listener can form a genuine intimacy, whether to sympathize, identify, quarrel, or share. In that sense I have been living with Beethoven's Quartet Op. 127 for a very long time, on intimate terms with it even when it is the furthest thing from my mind. The fact that such a musical work can never be fully present even in its richest appearance means that this intimacy cannot be closed and thus gives it grounds on which to thrive. The slight elusiveness that accompanies every performance is not a flaw, not a source of frustration, but a promise, a beckoning to listen on.

Part of the problem with the culture of classical music is that it receives all this with too much solemnity. It stifles its own energy with too much ceremony. But my experience with the Beethoven quartet was anything but ceremonious; it was visceral. And in that it was anything but unique. Being overwhelmed and shaken by a live performance is basic to the experience of such music. It seems doubtful that anyone could become fully absorbed in it without that experience to call on. The truth is that the quartet, for me, has always been whatever I heard that night, from which other encounters with both the score and its performances are greater or lesser departures. That, too, is anything but unique. So if we want to know why, and how, classical music still matters, we have to ask about the relationship of score and performance. We need to know what it means when the energy of performance releases the energy bound in the score. We need to know how the energy embodied in the score inspires the performer with the power to tap it and be touched, even transfigured, by it. We need to know where this energy comes from, whom it addresses, and what it has to offer us.

The search for answers will eventually lead to some deeply felt music heard, not in the concert hall, but at the movies. This won't happen for a while yet, but since the underlying connection may not be obvious, a trailer seemed a good idea. The rationale will come in due course, but, logic aside, the route is pleasant to follow. No one needs an excuse to enjoy a movie.

Performance is not supposed to affect the identity of a composition. It is not supposed to be able to. We can recognize a work of music whenever we encounter the notes as written in the score. We can hear it as something separate when it is transcribed, arranged, or adapted; we can hear it as somehow intact regardless of historical changes in instrument design, performance practice, sound recording, and the understanding of what fidelity to the score involves. The qualities of the work are supposed to be distinct from those of its performances. A particular performance may be boring, mediocre, exciting, revealing, transfiguring, and so on, but the music remains aloof. It is what it is in itself.

What would happen if we thought otherwise? If we regard the musical score not as the inscription of an unchanging work but rather as a dramatic scenario, a play- or shooting script, along lines recently suggested by Nicholas Cook, even the highly notated works that make up the classical canon change their character. If we accept a strong form of this argument, performance does not actualize or even interpret a prior musical "work" housed in notated patterns. Instead, the ways performance articulates and exceeds notation constitute what the music "is" for the occasion on which it is heard.

It therefore makes no sense to understand a score as a representation of an ideal musical work independent of the various performance styles that have been or may be applied to the score. The same is true of individual performances, which, whether because of their context or their character or some combination of both, can utterly change the meaning or even the very identity of the musical work. We have been trained not to admit this, but anyone who has ever heard a classical piece used in an advertisement has proof that it's true. And even in the concert or recital hall, the supposed work may not survive a lackluster or incompetent performance. It may not just "die" but not even be born.

Perhaps we should celebrate this. To anyone tired of the cult of the musical masterpiece, giving priority to performance is very appealing. It transfers authority from a gang of mummified Geniuses and their authorized representatives to a community of working and collaborating musicians. By doing so it also undercuts the tiresome claim of classical music to be timeless. What counts as a meaningful performance changes with changing times. Performance is irredeemably historical.

But then, so are scores. And it is doubtful whether performance can simply take over the authority traditionally invested in classical scores. The centrality of immutable, authoritative, notated patterns is an institutional fact about classical music, a part of its definition as a type. Without some prior interpretation of such patterns, even when they are obscure or ambiguous, the music simply won't come to life; it will just be a lively automaton.

The history of classical music is a history of practical idealization: of giving music an ideal form by treating it as if it had one. Throughout the nineteenth century, when the opportunity to hear orchestral music was rare, symphonies and concertos circulated widely in transcriptions for two pianos. People played and heard them for what was essential about the music, with which they often achieved an intimacy greater than anything available from later sound recordings of the full-dress versions. Such transcriptions, together with arrangements, occupy a gray area in which the musical work is both itself and not itself, present to the mind but absent to the senses.

Once recording began, the mind could fill in where the senses fell short. In the 78 rpm shellac recordings of the early twentieth century, the flat, scratchy sound of those same orchestral works and their regular interruption at four-minute intervals were largely a matter of indifference. People took the medium as transparent and marveled at the lifelikeness of the sound. In Thomas Mann's novel *The Magic Mountain* (1924), listeners to a phonograph on the eve of World War I "could scarcely believe their ears at the purity and faithful reproduction of the woodwind color. A solo violin preluded whimsically; the bowing, the *pizzicato*, the sweet gliding from one position to another, were all clearly audible. . . . The vivid, consummate piece of music was reproduced in all [its] richness." Mann's description might just as well have come from the 1924 catalog copy for the Victor Talking Machine Company's famous Victrola: "Any [model] will play your kind of music, and play it as it ought to be played. You may hear . . . the mighty strains of the symphony orchestra, the lone call of the forest songster, the thousand voices of the oratorio, [or] . . . the tremulous plea of the violin. . . . No distortion of tone is possible."

(My own first encounter with Beethoven's *Eroica* Symphony came in the basement of my grandparents' home, which contained a late-model Victrola in a tall mahogany cabinet, just my height. I liked to stick my head between the massive lid and the turntable as I wound the crank and set the heavy tone arm on the platter, as if to come as close as I could to Nipper, the Victor dog whose image adorned the body of the machine on a little plaque. The sound came out of that body at the level of my torso, magnified by opening a pair of doors the way one would lift a piano lid. The symphony's opening, two detached chords rapped out with neither ceremony nor apology, was thus literally visceral in its impact. To this day I can't hear the chords without feeling a touch of the gravelly old sound rising up from my midsection. The music may otherwise have made little conscious impression on me—I was only eight or nine—but the dropping of the platters certainly did, a dozen of them for the forty-five-minute recording. I expected each one to break as it fell, though none ever did. *That* was symphonic drama!)

The problem with making music ideal is the danger of idolizing it. Classical music lovers have no monopoly on this mistake, but the music has certainly suffered from it—precisely by coming to seem insufferable. That impression is perhaps the biggest noncommercial barrier to the health of classical music today. The time is long past when this music automatically commanded deference. It seems stuffy and outdated to too many people because we insist on walking on eggshells in its vicinity. We talk about it too timidly when we talk about it at all, and we listen to it too ceremoniously. We can no longer afford to do that, much less celebrate doing it. We don't want solemnity from music, at least outside funerals or memorials. We don't want the buttoned-up mannerisms of a bygone time. We want life.

Life: that's what the score and performance want from each other. The question of their relationship is not a matter of authority or hierarchy: Which is on top? Thinking of it that way is just a bad habit. The question, rather, is how a performance brings a score to life. And since life is changeful, unpredictable, often unfathomable, this is also the question of how a performance transforms a score by animating it. Galatea is never quite what Pygmalion imagines her to be. In turn this entails the complementary question of how a score—inanimate until sounded, even if only in memory or in a snatch of a tune hummed or whistled—imagines a kind of life to which it, and we, can aspire and to which any plausible performance must in some sense be answerable.

What's needed, in other words, is a means for understanding performance as simultaneously an act of creation and reproduction, a process that animates the spirit embedded in the ideal form of the score while at the same time reshaping that spirit in the act of bringing it to life. This is easy to say (what else would one say?), but it is hard to do and challenging to think about. Of course the formula is impossibly literal. Any actual performance will lean one way or the other, leave issues unresolved, exceed the mark here or default on it there. But this is not something to be regretted. Rather, it is precisely what keeps the score from hoarding too much or claiming too little authority. If we adopt as a goal, both as listeners and, if we play, as performers, the ideal of consulting the score but not venerating it, interpreting its fixed features without mystifying them, the results, though inevitably imperfect, will carry the marks of our involvement, our values, our feelings, and our understanding. And these are the marks we need to find in the music for it to find us where we live.

This search is shaped by the unexpected force of a simple fact we have met with before but by no means exhausted. The performance is supposed to repeat the composition in every detail—every single one. As we've also noted, just what this mandate means has changed over time along with performance practices, aesthetic values, and technology, but the underlying ideal has remained reasonably—indeed, remarkably—durable. The expectation of this all-embracing repetition is transformative. It creates the frame of reference within which the music's details come to matter, in which they become rich with significance the way a color deepens in just the right light or a sensation of warmth or excitement or desire spreads over the surface of the body. In part the composer crafts the detail to do this; in part the expectation of repetition, plus the memory of it, plus the desire for it, elicits the latent power of detail to do this and thus guides the composer's hand.

The relationship between the ideal and the actual forms of the music, between the musical score and its performances, is essential to this effect. This relationship is paradoxical. It cannot be otherwise. The performances must realize the music exactly, in the sense that they are expected to comply with whatever the score explicitly requires. But they must never do so in just one way. Ideally speaking, no two performances should sound just alike. The music ideally embodied by the classical score has an identity, even a personality, but it has no location, no material form. It is—does not "express" but is—spirit, energy, impulse, yet unlike these other impalpable, half-metaphoric entities the music has a definite character that we can revisit as often as we like: as long, that is, as we can change the music in the act of reproducing it note for note. The identity of classical music lives by difference and only by difference. The difference constantly returns it to itself. The score is like a map that traces a route while erasing its destination.

To create this situation it is not enough just to write down all the notes. What makes a score "classical" is the particular relationship between the way it is written and the way it is treated. The classical score has to project a conception of the fate of melody (or a credible alternative), and it has to endow its details with meaning and drama. The feeling of what happens musically has to energize the combination of exactitude and difference that guides the performance of the score. The performance at the same time has to energize the feeling of what happens musically. This mutuality is the basis on which the score seeks to embody something—something singular—that we desire to hear reanimated and reinterpreted, not just reproduced, by successive performances. The classical work is not one that accepts change from note-for-note performance but one that seeks it. What it risks in being performed is not becoming different but staying the same.

It is important not to misunderstand this point. Not all performances are dramatically different, though subtle differences are not hard to find. And the principle of difference in the performance of a score has nothing to do with clichés about the inexhaustibility of great art. The principle applies to stupid or boring works as well as to enthralling ones. It arises from historical changes wrought by custom and technology as well as from differences of individual interpretation. What matters, and makes the music matter, is that every performance sounds against an imaginary backdrop of others, some convergent with it, some divergent or oblique, some antagonistic. The music must be the same, the performances not. When the performances interpret, they represent the music's meaning, not just its notes. The very act of doing so helps bring the meaning into being. And where meaning is concerned, one interpretation entails a network of others. To perform the music is not just to represent it but to position it.

Something of this positioning is lost in the more literal repetition afforded by recordings, but less than one might think. The positioning is part of what is recorded. A classical performance always addresses the listener against the possibility or memory of other note-for-note renditions. Vernacular music has no equivalent to this; it has other virtues. The vernacular "classic" is a particular recording that can only be reproduced technologically; its melody can be endlessly adapted or rearranged, but there is no "work" that can be "performed." (There is a product that can be copyrighted, but that is another story.) Contrariwise, a classical composition cannot have a "cover"—industry jargon for the rerecording by one pop star or group of another's hit song. Classical performance animates a score on behalf of the player or listener; vernacular performance animates itself with the help of a musical number. There are exceptions and overlaps—as always, with anything—but those are the facts of the matter and the sources of what matters.

Classical music occupies its own special mode of time, which comes about only in the mutual embrace of score and performance. The time is utopian, a condition that either the score or the performance can either simply embody or reflect on by the way it proceeds. In a poem about a deep, lingering tone, Rainer Maria Rilke once described music as "lasting pressed from passing," like juice from an orange or oil from olives. Nicholas Cook echoes the idea when he speaks of music as an "imaginary object" seeking to "snatch a moment of eternity from the jaws of evanescence." The fixed notes of classical music allow the passing of time to become its own antidote. Each new performance reenacts a bygone event as if it were happening for the first time; the exactitude of the passing is the source of the lasting. In this regard the classical composition is the complement of the jazz improvisation. Where the latter fills out a specific duration in a unique manner, the former creates something paradoxical, a repeatable uniqueness, which, again paradoxically, requires for its live realization a unique and special occasion. This feature of the music gives its performance, especially in longer, more ambitious pieces where an appreciable amount of time is involved, the aspect of ritual or of festive observance.

What changes, then, from one classical performance to another? Pace, touch, tempo, color, phrasing, voice, texture, emphasis—the list is long. But it is not only such differences in the manner and means of performance that count. It is also the circumstances of the performance, be they personal (my encounter with the Beethoven quartet) or communal (the Brahms Requiem in the wake of 9/11). The music absorbs those circumstances from all quarters, diffuses them throughout its melodic drama and richly detailed articulation, and makes them a part of itself.

Perhaps the most vital role for performance in this process is precisely to suggest verbal and imagistic connections with the world, the very thing that the traditional culture of classical music, in the twentieth century at any rate, tried to get us to regard as forbidden. Thinking in these terms encourages us to hear a given performance more fully in light of how it positions itself vis-à-vis both the score and other performances, possible and actual. You can find out a good deal about what music means by asking what a performance does and doesn't do and how it might have acted otherwise. The performer's activity may indeed resemble that of an actor reading a script, but it may resemble many other things as well: the intonation of an authoritative word; a speaker trying to evade censorship in both the political and the Freudian senses of the term; a person trying to formulate a memory or describe a scene; or someone applying a text learned by heart to a new situation.

This is not an exhaustive list. Take those opening chords in Beethoven's Quartet Op. 127: I have heard some ensembles tear headlong into them as if trying to live up to an impossible demand, and I have heard others take them as a license to dwell on the pure sensuous pleasure of harmonious sound. Neither was the way they sounded (the way they were played? the way I heard them?) on the night I described earlier, when they seemed to rise up from an almost frightening depth of serenity.

Regardless of the specific analogies involved, thinking about the performer or performance in the sense of creative reproduction and worldly activity takes us into the wider field of human performances, both symbolic and material, and therefore into the realms of action, desire, social condition, and the vitality of experience. It directs us to the often trying, but deeply rewarding, marriage of the character of performance and the characteristics of the thing performed, neither of which has the first word—or the last.

What does this marriage look—or sound—like? If one were to imagine a handbook of the meeting of work and performance, what would it include? Some of the entries might read like this:

Virtually all performances are performances *of* something, even if that something becomes something else in being performed.

The pure performance event would be one that vanishes in the moment of its creation without the possibility of description or recording. A performance freezes into a work the moment someone describes it or the moment it becomes repeatable in a recording medium. A work unfreezes into a performance the moment someone reads or hears or sees it, or even imagines or remembers it; its pattern moves and transforms itself while also standing still.

A performance needs the work it may exceed or transform; a work needs a performance to exceed or transform it.

Works that don't change in performance are dead; performances that don't convey what's unchanging in a work are deadly.

Works perform or not; performances work or not.

Works and performances have no relationship, only relationships.

A thirty-minute work can sometimes be performed in three—minutes or seconds.

This last epigram may seem strange. We need to dwell on it. Not all performances of a work need to be full or faithful to it, as long as *some* are, or may be. What matters is not that I always listen to all of a piece with full attention but that I sometimes do, and have, and may again. These possibilities depend on each other. The partial performances—adaptations, condensations, imitations, reminiscences, and so on—may be the more prevalent. They are the means by which everyday life absorbs the power of art. It is because of this that partial performances in and by film, the dominant medium of the modern era, are so rich in significance. The full performances are set apart. They are like pastoral interludes, contemplative retreats from the messy business of living, but their pastoral idea is not an escape from reality; it is a link between one reality and another. Listening intently to a few full performances as time and conditions allow is valuable not just for its intrinsic satisfactions but for the possibility of a ripple effect that spreads far as it lasts long.

Once I get a feeling for how classical music goes—once I've learned a little and heard rather more—I can hear this music in fragments large or small with keen appreciation. And in a real sense what I hear is "all" of it. The music sounds within a complex memory-space that looks both before and after, that projects both the sound and the meaning of the music forward and backward in time and into all the reaches of cultural space. It can do this equally well if it arrests my ongoing activities or just goes along with them. Some pieces can live for years on the slenderest of diets. Some can thrive on the basis of a few synoptic bars to be hummed or sung or recalled; Beethoven's Quartet Op. 127 has thrived that way for me ever since the night, the season, it illuminated long ago. Such music expands and contracts its full extent with limitless flexibility and without substantial loss. What matters in classical music is not the fullness of its statement, pleasurable as that can be, but the fullness of its kind and content, the forces and visions that it discloses in the intimate space of listening.

It makes no sense, then, to think of classical music purely in terms of works—the traditional way, and the one whose stultifying effects we're trying to escape. But it makes no sense, either, to believe that performance can simply rescue us from the tyranny of the work, or that idealizing performance is any better or less tyrannical than idealizing the work. What does make sense is to recognize that classical music asks its listeners to imagine a work with more fullness and complexity than most other music does; that it invites them to contemplate, with the same fullness and complexity, the work they have imagined; and that this process is animating rather than ossifying when it is intimately connected to the realities and possibilities of performances both full and partial, in an ever-unfinished network of contexts and uses. The old, quasi-sacramental idea of performance as pure realization is out of gas (or rather, alas, it isn't). Classical music still matters because we can now openly recognize something that has always been true of it but little heeded: that performance is a way to live with music, and even a little to live through music, and that anyone and everyone can play.

How to explore the rich relationships, in both life and music, intimated by these remarks? Perhaps the best way to understand the re-creative role of performance in linking the work and the world is to study specific examples of it. Such examples are readily found in literature, drama, and film, which often give moments of musical performance an epitomizing, even a transformative value. Drama and film regularly represent acts of performance. They show and ponder the very thing they're made of, the acting and enacting that are as basic to social life as they are to dramatic art.

When these performances are musical, they have the special value of bridging the gap between fiction and reality. The musical performances may occur in a fictional world, but they themselves are real. We don't hear an imitation of the music; we hear the thing itself. Like the principle of performing the classical score note for note, this simple fact has wide repercussions. One of the reasons that music in drama or film is taken as a pledge of emotional truth is that its expressive presence is the one unimpeachably true thing in a purely illusory world. It may be used to deceive or manipulate us, but its presence cannot be deceptive. We believe in music because if we can hear it, it must be real. Music cannot be impersonated. Musical theater and opera rely on this reality effect, too; they tend to foster an awareness of themselves as ritual occasions on which to witness singing. Musical theater is the art of making us hearken.

Film in particular, from its earliest days, gathered the tendencies of the older media together and found an enduring fascination in the power of musical performance both shown on screen and heard off screen.

The filmic instances also make it plain that the emotional or semantic richness of a musical performance does not depend on its completeness. Performances are often adaptive or fragmentary in both life and art and are none the less authentic for it. They may not give all the music, but whatever they give is all there. I can be as moved by humming a melody or overhearing a snatch of opera on the radio as I am by listening absorbedly to a whole work or attending a performance at the opera house. Sometimes I'm even more moved by the fragment or adaptation.

Film counts heavily on this power of classical performance to remain—to become—numinous when compressed.

Another thing one quickly learns from the movies is that what the performance puts at stake is very often the possibility of tapping into a source of life-enhancing social energy. Classical music shares this potential with more vernacular types. This chapter will go on to discuss several films that depend on performances of classical music to defeat joylessness, intolerance, hypocrisy, and worse, but there is no patent to be had on this purpose. In Joel and Ethan Coen's reworking of the Odyssey in Depression-era Mississippi, *Oh Brother, Where Art Thou* (2000), the decisive event is a rousing performance of Delta blues that routs the Ku Klux Klan. But the extravagance of this counterexample has its own tale to tell. Classical music knows better than to strain credulity. It takes greater risks as it takes in darker knowledge, which gives both its power to lament and its power to celebrate a distinctive value available nowhere else.

This special value is hard to specify, and perhaps the better for being so. It has something to do with the sense—we've met with it before and will again—that more is at stake in a classical performance than a correct or even compelling execution of the notes. The performance translates the fixed shape of the work into a flowing motion; it animates the work by submitting the certainties of a pattern to the uncertainties of experience. When we hear it that way, we also hear a demonstration of the possibility of continually reanimating the things we know and value, of vesting new meanings in them as old ones erode or go bad. Performing the music in new contexts and connections, with the expressive choices appropriate to them, opens new possibilities of meaning. These are possibilities that the music not only receives but also gives. It gives them as the particular rendition of the score takes its place amid the memory and possibility of other renditions. And it gives them as the performance at hand confronts the internal logic of the musical pattern that every performance must honor in the course of extending and transforming it.

The films to illustrate these points come in two pairs, drawn from historical moments roughly forty years apart. The broad time span is meant to suggest continuities in the way classical music matters amid changing historical circumstances—the very quality claimed by the overworked term *classical*. The films are in part about that too. The more recent examples deal with the past, the musical world of which holds something valuable that the present has lost. The older examples deal with their own present, in which music gives or withholds the possibilities of the future. In order of discussion, the films are James Lapine's historical romance *Impromptu* (1991), Bruce Beresford's historical drama *Paradise Road* (1997), David Lean and Noel Coward's romantic melodrama *Brief Encounter* (1946), and Joseph Mankeiwicz's romantic comedy *People Will Talk* (1951, two years before the director's *Julius Caesar*, and tellingly so, given the Shakespearian mode of the earlier film).

Each of these films focuses on the way music is transmitted as well as the way it is performed, and each does so in a symbolically resonant setting. *Impromptu* dwells on the piano as the nineteenth-century version of a broadcast medium; the principal setting is a country house, a scene of nostalgia for the nineteenth century's unembarrassed worship of genius and high culture. *Paradise Road* dramatizes the transcription of orchestral scores for unaccompanied women's chorus in a prisoner-of-war camp, a site in which deprivation evolves through music into an opportunity for a kind of heroic tinkering. *Brief Encounter* links the radio, narrative memory, and the film's soundtrack. Its narrative centers on a train station, the site of transit, transition, transitoriness: qualities with a key bearing on the mores and morals of life in the aftermath of World War II. Those things also bear directly on the university setting of *People Will Talk*, the site where old ideas and values are both preserved and challenged. The film's romantic plot depends on a radio broadcast of Wagner, its dramatic plot on a performance of Brahms by the university orchestra.

All four films are exemplary in engaging both score and performance, the life imagined and the life realized or—the case of *Brief Encounter* and *Paradise Road*—both realized and thwarted. All are in some sense about the theme of this volume, the value of a score-based music in an age or generation that postdates its composition. And all are to be understood, not as merely using or adapting the music, but as performing it in a context that animates potentials for meaning the music has never failed to have, before or since. Film, too, is a mode of performance. And in our media-saturated age it is a very important one, as ubiquitous in its way as the parlor piano was in the nineteenth century. These days the film is often running on a wide screen right where the piano used to be, as the parlor replaces the movie house by which it was once replaced.

The four films are at one level a miscellany, a series of illustrations only, but at another level they form a strangely coherent group. Each of the two historical moments from which they date represents a period of relative calm before an unanticipated crisis: the midcentury films before the Korean War and nuclear arms race, the late-century films before September 11 and the new reign of terror. The music in each, both as score and as performance, becomes a means of harnessing a utopian social energy in a moment shortly before such a thing will come to seem impossible. The films address dilemmas that seem capable of resolution by acts of will or good faith, in a spirit that calls a community into being by preserving rather than correcting the distinctiveness, even the quirkiness, of individuals.

Impromptu retells the romantic legend of Chopin and George Sand. Its tone is witty and irreverent, but the film can barely conceal its fondness for an age in which it was possible to believe in true art, art uncorrupted by commercial or social pressures, even though the pressures were palpable on all sides. This artistic integrity proves itself by creating an unlikely romance and, through music, fostering a renovation of sexuality. The nineteenth-century music of Chopin becomes a covert vehicle of late-twentieth-century idealism about art, sexuality, and society—an idealism no longer possible to proclaim directly.

Circumventing that impossibility is also one of the purposes of *Paradise Road*, which finds its own cover for idealism, and for heroism, by dramatizing a true story from the war that forms the silent background for *Brief Encounter* and *People Will Talk*. Its subject is a group of women from several nations interred in Sumatra by the Japanese for four years. At first in secret, then in defiance of their captors, the women transcribed a series of classical scores from memory and formed a choral "orchestra" to perform the music in the camp. In this case, the utopian space created by music was not metaphorical.

Brief Encounter is about the possibility of escape from a joyless marriage, reflective of the drab spirit of a nominally victorious nation still reeling from the devastation of the war. The attempt is a failure, a hollow triumph for a repressive social order, but the failure transcends the order that imposes it and the lost romance survives in the very memory, narrative, and music that record its loss.

People Will Talk is about the possibility of marriage itself as a means of liberation from repressive order; it operates in the spirit of the brief interwar moment when America, the real victor in 1945, seems to have inherited the earth. The music in the film is a celebration of new beginnings, one in the sphere of marriage, another in the sphere of community; both spheres witness a triumph over tin ears and hard hearts.

The source of the energy, vitality, and longing that at the best imbue the ritual or festive dimension of the music heard in these films is a performative freedom that links the musical experience to a wider imaginative freedom regarded as a birthright. This is the freedom celebrated by the Enlightenment subject, the person imagined and historically formed by the tradition from which classical music primarily hails. Self-denying discipline and obedience to the master—whether conductor or composer—is not of the essence of this music but a later historical contingency best left to wither away. What remains we can see on screen. The pull of festivity and ritual, the balance of fidelity and freedom, and the revival of classical music as the friend of free but also sociable subjectivity—all are basic to our four films, whose new run starts now.

The first half of *Impromptu* takes place on the estate of a Philistine count and his culture-starved wife, who has brought in a raft of celebrated artists—Sand, Delacroix, and the poet Alfred de Musset as well as both Chopin and Liszt—to render an otherwise boring life meaningful. The film satirizes this typically modern aspiration through the contrast between the idyllic pastoral surroundings and the buffoonery that dominates the house party. Only Sand and Chopin understand that art enhances life only indirectly, by suggestion, never by program or pronouncement. Chopin's music, presented as indifferent to its socially cushy surroundings even though Chopin himself is knowingly dependent on them, becomes the object of Sand's desire because it embodies the power of indirect enrichment. Chopin is less the maker of his music than its personification.

At one point Chopin and Liszt sit at the piano together and play a four-hand duet; the scene is intercut with the plotting of a bedroom-farce deception involving a stolen letter. The music that the composers play is a transcription from Beethoven's *Pastoral* Symphony. The third movement of this work is a country dance; its title, "Merry Gathering of the Country Folk," conveys what the fictional Chopin and Liszt are seeking in it. They want to be playful, even a bit foolish, but they want to retain their integrity as musicians, too. Amid the farcical goings-on of the house party, the music, with its evocation of rustic festivity, takes on an ideal sturdiness and authenticity. It evokes the pastoral world in which the guests ought to participate, but can't, because their own world of debased modernity depends on its extinction. The only place the true pastoral world can survive—or, what amounts to the same thing, come into being—is in the obvious, childish, socially oblivious excitement shared by Chopin and Liszt as they play. Their musical culture, together with their shared automatic assumption that Beethoven is the acme and center of that culture—historically an assumption true to Liszt but quite false to Chopin—momentarily carries them away from the modern world of pretentious malice, social and sexual corruption, and empty chatter about the magnificence of art.

This self-conscious pastoral makes the two great composers giddy and even goofy, very much like the children that the film recurrently shows making mischief knowingly while the adults do it blindly. Shoulder to shoulder, glance to glance, Chopin and Liszt enjoy a physical as well as a cultural intimacy. At the end, they quickly rise from their seats, switch places, and exchange parts to play the final cadence—after which they hug each other. This marks the last moment in the film when the two men are close in any sense: the power and the limits of nostalgia could not be more clearly defined. But only the *Pastoral* Symphony could define them. Even in the 1830s, the film rightly suggests, no other work could legitimize nostalgia as this one could. (Chapter 6 will revisit this topic, and this music, in greater depth.) Written just a generation earlier, the *Pastoral* Symphony already seemed to belong to an older and better world, even though its own pastoral vision was already anachronistic. Only the *Pastoral* could support the fantasy through which Liszt and Chopin, in an instant, become the Gemini twins of a mystical musical collective.

The film's Chopin makes this point, too. In a later scene, solo this time, he accompanies a playlet by Musset based on Noah's flood. The music again comes from the *Pastoral* Symphony: the first raindrops of the storm that disrupts the country dance. This musical image resonates here with Chopin's own so-called Raindrop Prelude, which the composer has played earlier—this is the film's little joke—on a dismally rainy day. (Modern rain is depressing, even when Chopin portrays it; in this case it even drives his art-infatuated hostess to an exasperated outburst.) But when the playlet turns out to be a cruel satire on his hosts,

Chopin interrupts the performance. He refuses to let the nostalgic authority of Beethoven condone the smug sense of superiority assumed by the band of the artists. His refusal amounts to a withdrawal of nostalgia itself, the only thing that can give any sense to the contagious idiocy all around him.

But the film restores the nostalgia that its Chopin retracts. The only difference between the theatrical performance put on by the characters and the movie we are watching is the technology involved. *Impromptu* is a self-reflective work. The viewer's relation to the world of the film reduplicates the relation of the film's Chopin and Liszt to the world of Beethoven. We, the audience, long for the romantic extravagance embodied by the film's characters as they themselves long for the pastoral innocence embodied by the *Pastoral* Symphony. And for that we need not Beethoven's music but Chopin's, with which Sand falls in love before she ever sees the composer. Because she chooses to act on her fantasy—she climbs through Chopin's window like a burglar when she hears him playing the lyrical climax to his Ballade in G Minor—the music becomes a means to free Chopin from prudery and Sand from cynical world-weariness.

The two eventually consummate their relationship to an orchestrated version of this extract on the soundtrack. The orchestration draws the music outside the strict high-culture orbit into the realm of romantic underscoring that all moviegoers know well. It turns the Ballade into a fragmentary Romantic concerto, a type we will meet again, more authentically, in *Brief Encounter.* Chopin's music, among the most popular and popularized of the classics, as well as the most distinctive in its expressiveness, shifts effortlessly between realms. Its orchestration can voice satisfaction as richly as its original version could voice desire. This versatility tells us that we can have our Chopin as we want and need him to be; we can play him any way we like.

The nostalgia in *Paradise Road* is not for music, though music is its medium; it is for heroism. The film is interesting in part because it flirts openly with cliché. The women's Japanese captors are infinitely cruel (especially the one who speaks perfect English); the masterpieces of Western music exalt the captives and touch the hard hearts of their guards—clear proof of the superiority of Western civilization. Yet the film is based on actual events. The cruelty was real; the singing was real; the movie uses the actual arrangements made by the women in the camp.

Two of these are performed. Each is an extract from a larger piece but entirely faithful in melody, harmony, and rhythm. In each, the musical adaptation conveys a rich message by both what it contains and what it omits. At one level, the women seek solace in the music's beauty, energy, and design. At another, they express the truth about their captivity through the music's meaning, but in a form their captors cannot understand.

The first extract is from Antonin Dvorak's *New World* Symphony, written in the United States in 1893 in the spirit, so Dvorak said, of native and African American folk melody. The women sing the choralelike prelude and first and second themes of the slow movement. Here as in the symphony the center of gravity is the first theme, originally composed for English horn. The plaintive melody is independently famous. Dvorak's student, Harry Burleigh, adapted it as a spiritual, "Goin' Home," and its affinity with the style of the spirituals allows it to tap into their deep longing for homecoming, salvation, relief from a weary load.

The resonance with the captives' plight is clear to everyone but their captors, who can hear nothing in the music but its beauty.

As the women sing, the melody becomes a wordless hymn, a transformation already begun in the prelude. But a greater transformation is to come. The second theme turns to a minor key; it is agitated in its sorrow where the first is tranquil. In the symphony this portends a dialogue and eventual reconciliation between the themes, but in the prison camp it marks an end: a dead stop. The women edit the music to revoke the fate of melody. They will not be reconciled to their captivity, and as they sing the agitation of the second theme becomes an expression of anger and defiance that they will *not* revoke. Their recalcitrance becomes explicit after the concert when they refuse to sing a Japanese folk song as an encore—and get away with it.

The second extract is from Maurice Ravel's *Bolero* (1928), a "gamble" of a piece according to its composer, in which the same music returns over and over amid changes of orchestration in a long crescendo that peaks, just before the close, in a moment of orgiastic furor. The women's performance ventures further toward the expression of defiance by giving a martial touch to the omnipresent rhythm of the bolero (an impassioned Spanish dance, normally for couples). The voices join in a sharp articulation, *bum-buppity bum-bum-bum-bum*, pouncing aggressively on the consonants. The sound suggests the rattle of imaginary artillery, especially as the crescendo mounts.

But with that the women reach their limit. They can reproduce a portion of Ravel's music note for note—the film briefly shows us the handwritten score, so that we see as well as hear the liberating movement from score to performance—but they cannot reproduce his paroxysm of a climax. They have neither the resources, nor the time, nor the energy. They are, after all, half-starved. So their performance also expresses a futility that the film itself declines to acknowledge. In real life half the singers died in captivity, and the music stopped when the ranks thinned to that point; the rest were too debilitated to go on. A few beautiful shots of graves in the rain are not adequate to register this. Neither, perhaps, is the gap in the music. But for those who know *Bolero* (or for anyone who can imagine what must be coming) the paradoxical presence-in-absence of the wild, dissonant, bacchanalian outburst offers the fuller acknowledgment.

Brief Encounter has nothing to say about the heroics of the war that moves *Paradise Road* so much; it is too close to care. The film tells a familiar tale of doomed adulterous love. A dissatisfied housewife meets a dashing, idealistic doctor during a weekly commute; their encounters become increasingly ardent but fall just short of consummation before the doctor, in moral flight, takes a job abroad and the wife returns to her stolid husband. We have seen it all before. The only new wrinkle is that the wife, Laura, gets to be guilty without having been happy. But the story takes on unusual poignancy because the object of its longing is not so much an ideal love as the premodern, prewar world in which ideal love seemed possible. The film's opening is close to explicit about this. Laura is not only the film's protagonist but also its narrator. When we see her first her affair is already over. She is sitting with her husband and listening to the radio. Then, fatefully, she turns the radio dial from jazz or swing to the Rachmaninoff Second Piano Concerto and finds herself impelled to tell her story. The music is half a century old; the story is older still.

This moment encapsulates everything to follow. What we see in the film corresponds to Laura's narrative, addressed mentally to her husband; the movie audience hears her unspoken thoughts. What Laura herself hears is the concerto, which is concurrent with her story; the film ends with the ending of the music. We understand that the concerto speaks for her in her voice's stead; it breaks through on the soundtrack at moments of peak feeling.

Broadcast live, the performance freezes for Laura, and for us, into the sound of a higher-order music box. It becomes a casket to contain the desire for life in the larger sense that she can never fulfill, except in the still-potent medium of this very music. The music contains the narrative we see and also the one we don't, the one with the new couple fulfilling their romance. The role of the music is to defer the moment at which the second narrative must submit to the first. But the music can do that only by curbing its own unrealized possibilities. In the world of the film, this concerto, which can always be performed another way, will not and cannot be performed in any way other than the one we hear. Part of its power—and the film, a famous tearjerker, would surely leave many eyes drier without it—comes from the music's being trapped by a narrative in which it refuses to believe.

But why just this music? Why this Romantic piano concerto, the very acme of the type?

For just that reason. In the Romantic concerto the piano encounters an "objective" expression of feeling in the orchestra and proceeds to make it "subjective"—internal, personal, authentic, deep—by combining it with expressions of response: rippling scales and arpeggios; countermelodies, often in inner voices; enrichments of texture; sensuous chord progressions; changes of harmony. The resulting dialogue is the defining characteristic of the genre. It depends on carefully preserving both the objective and subjective perspectives, neither of which is meaningful without the other: the objective lacking meaning, the subjective lacking reference. But the balance is not a clockwork device or a reconciliation of opposites; the genre takes it as a means, not as an end. The end lies precisely in the transformation of objective givens to subjective truth. In most Romantic concertos, and certainly in this one, the process goes on unimpeded. The genre helps create and uphold the dream, the myth, of a deep subjectivity immune from manipulation or constraint by external forces.

In Laura's world, such music is an anachronism, laden with feelings that have long since lost their credibility. Yet nothing could be more timely, even more modern. The music is no mere accessory to her story: it is that story. The events she narrates are just illustrations. The concerto belongs to a vanished world, one that predates the media—both radio and film—that convey it. It represents the survival of that world as a lost possibility, or more exactly as an impossibility. More than that, its own romantic longing, in its own day, is already nostalgia for a lost world, perhaps the very one envisioned in its immediate predecessor in this vein, the Tchaikovsky First Concerto. For Laura the music stands in the place of memories and secrets, and in its technological reproducibility it satisfies the desire whose loss it predicts and laments. It turns modernity against itself. Its liberating energy conflicts with the pathos of Laura's narrative, but unlike Laura it does not surrender its drive. Its refusal is what makes the film moving.

At the end, Laura contemplates throwing herself under a train, but does not; she is a failed Anna Karenina, second-rate in her tepid modernity. Yet the (Russian) music retains the Tolstoyan grandeur that Laura renounces, and the very act of telling her story—not to the husband who never hears her (in any sense) but to her peers in the movie house, those who identify with her desire—upholds a utopian hope in the guise of the music.

In making this possible, the film gets the music exactly right. The concerto becomes more itself, more audibly itself, for its usage in the film. It becomes both what it has always been and what it has not yet been, while always retaining the power to become something else. This music is profoundly paradoxical, and the rifts at its core bespeak some long-standing rifts in worldly life: between social constraint and desire, and between transcendental longing and material reality.

The music is socially accommodating. Broadcast on the radio as an alternative to jazz, it belongs to the norms of respectable life, at home (literally, thanks to the radio) in the status quo. If there is something wrong with it, for all its expressive warmth and its wealth of the pianistic textures by which the Romantic concerto seeks to deepen and enrich the possibilities of feeling, the problem is that the fate of melody in this music is too secure and too lucky, even in its melancholy. Nothing can make the tunes less than glorious. Yet it is just this security that allows the music to overrun the emotional and social borders that contain it and insist on something better. The music ruptures social accommodation from within and offers itself as a surrogate for the passions and pleasures stinted by the world to which it nominally conforms itself.

So, too, with the romantic longing that permeates the music and guides the return of its melodies, which approach but never achieve a moment of perfect self-sufficiency. The music seems to aim at more than the world, any world, modern or not, can give. Like many nineteenth-century romantic narratives—*Anna*

Karenina again comes to mind—it takes romantic feeling as a portal to something higher. Yet it does so with a sensuous lushness that is its own reward, its own answer to the supposedly transcendental desire. It creates a material fabric that is sheer pleasure to the touch and, as the metaphor suggests, erotically charged. As it should be: one should never forget that the unspoken—and unconsummated—bliss of *Brief Encounter* belongs to sex.

People Will Talk exactly reverses the values of *Brief Encounter.* It makes the reward of a conventionally illicit love a happy marriage and suggests that the chief barrier to a rewarding future is a peculiarly joyless brand of Philistinism that no one needs to embrace.

Like its Shakespearean models, the film's plot unites its lovers against the will of a narrow-minded antagonist and in the process revives the spirit of community. The details are too elaborate to summarize; suffice it to say that the film—defying F. Scott Fitzgerald's famous claim that there are no second acts in American life—is about second chances, the promise of pregnancy, figurative rebirths, and even a virtual waking of the dead. Throughout, the energy of life triumphs over restrictive custom and law, a point the central romance makes bluntly. A young woman, pregnant by a lover who has abandoned her, sinks into suicidal despair; an idealistic doctor and professor revives her spirits, the two promptly fall in love, and—after wooing each other in a cowshed, of which more anon—they unite in marriage and symbolically unite the community through music.

The music is the Academic Festival Overture of Brahms, which frames the film in multiple ways: as title music, as theme music, in rehearsal near the beginning, in performance at the conclusion. For the conclusion to come about, the doctor, Noah Praetorius, must get through a McCarthy-style inquisition at the university, instigated by his antagonist, Professor Elwell; the hearing is holding up the start of the concert, which Praetorius is to conduct. The music acts as a portrait of everything Praetorius embodies and Elwell denies.

Characters first; and in this case the actors are important. Praetorius is an inimitable blend of sage and schoolboy, pomposity and ardor; he might be said to combine the qualities of Hans Sachs and Walther von Stolzing in Wagner's opera *Die Meistersinger*, the film's other point of musical reference (it's in that cowshed). His effect on other people is consistently to charm their spirits, to bring them back to life in one sense or another. (He succeeds precisely where Laura's love interest, also an idealistic doctor, fails.) He is, in short, Cary Grant, who plays him. Elwell is a mean-spirited gnome, brilliantly played by Hume Cronyn as hunched, shuffling, uncomfortable in his own skin. His name is a pun on Ill-Will, the same as that of his prototype, the Malvolio of Shakespeare's *Twelfth Night*, whose rebuke to tuneful carousing, rebutted by the famous question "Dost thou think, because thou art virtuous, there will be no more cakes and ale?" is the pivot on which the film turns. Elwell also has a touch of Shylock in him, not as a Jew but as a fellow music-hater, the faintly reptilian curmudgeon who shuts the window on the joyous sounds of Brahms at the start of the film and who, at the end, declines to open the door that would bring him into both the concert and the community.

Elwell, who is so remote from life and desire that he can't even drink a glass of water offered him by Anne, newly married to Praetorius, also forms a parody of a romantic union. His partner is none other than the Wicked Witch of the West: Margaret Hamilton, who played the role in *The Wizard of Oz* and who alludes to it by saying sharply that she hasn't changed much since the 1930s, which is more or less true. This character disappears after the opening scenes, as if she were—melting.

In contrast to the standard Hollywood-comedy association of classical music with characters like Elwell, *People Will Talk* associates it with the energy that perpetuates life, the wit and passion that "makes sick people well." Brahms's Overture combines a rambunctious, playful energy, especially notable in bumptious rub-a-dub-dub patter on the lower strings, which figures prominently in the film, with a warm romantic lyricism; it also combines learned formal techniques with traditional student songs, genially mocking the sententiousness of the one and the rowdiness of the other. The best known of the songs, reserved for a conclusion of unapologetic grandeur, is "Gaudeamus Igitur" (Let's Rejoice Now), the text of which sums up the themes of the film: "Let's rejoice now / While we're young, / After joyous youth, / After joyless age, / The dust will have us." The film takes this message literally. The joy it projects is found not in the music, abstractly regarded, but in the rehearsal and performance of the music as shared in a moment of festivity by the whole community.

And the film says so. Brahms, in 1880, assumed that his audience would hear the words unsung behind the music. The film takes the liberty of adding them. As Praetorius exuberantly waves his baton, the concert concludes as a chorus of students stands and sings "Gaudeamus Igitur." At that, the overture literally becomes an Ode to Joy, picking up the mode and role of Beethoven's Ninth Symphony—as we might have guessed it would. Noah Praetorius has a secret (well, several). His real first name is Ludwig.

What Brahms is to community, meanwhile, his old antagonist Wagner is to romance. The music here is the Prize Song from *Die Meistersinger,* the love song by which the hero, Walther, achieves his artistic maturity and wins his bride. The music is subtly designed both to reconcile the principles of artistic and romantic aspiration and to trace the curve of rising ardor. It enters the film via the radio at the farmhouse of Anne's Elwell-like uncle, where Praetorius has followed her, but unlike the Rachmaninoff concerto of *Brief Encounter* this music has real-world effects. It migrates to the soundtrack as Anne and Praetorius take a tour of the farm's milking shed to examine the state-of-the-art equipment. As the two babble on about milking, each one trying to disavow being head-over-heels in love with the other, the music that neither of them hears stands in the place of their desire and voices it with a passion to which they both, in the end, succumb with relief. Their babble becomes a duet in which unconscious musical performance becomes romantic consummation. ("Don't mess with the unconscious," Anne says later, meaning: let it do its work. Let it tell you when to come to your senses by losing them.)

The film uses no other music but the Brahms and Wagner. That it does so is telling—and assumes a degree of cultural literacy in the audience that ought to be possible again today with our superior media capacities. That the music should speak for romantic and social freedom in 1951, well into the postwar Red Scare and on the cusp of the McCarthy era, is even more telling. The concluding performance, especially with its Ninth Symphony allusion suggesting an all-embracing joy from which one may only, like Elwell and his namesake Malvolio, be self-excluded, affirms a culture of transformative play in which law and desire, like energy and lyricism or student songs and the fate of melody, are reconciled without loss to either. Within the limits of its historical moment (we have to accept a privileged white community as a symbol for community in general), the performance finds the same utopian hope in this music that *Brief Encounter* despairs of in Rachmaninoff, *Paradise Road* tries to recapture in Dvorak and Ravel, and *Impromptu* fantasizes about regaining through Beethoven and Chopin.

And now a coda. Three of our four films contain moments in which music and language trade places. All are moments of special intensity or truth, moments at which the passage from score to performance is especially fraught. In each case, the musical performance spills over into the performance of a key narrative action. *People Will Talk* gives us the gleaming orchestration and sensuous line of Wagner's Prize Song, but the song remains unsung; instead we hear the spoken "arias" of Anne and Praetorius, to which the song forms the unconscious they're not supposed to mess with. At a pivotal moment of *Brief Encounter* the Rachmaninoff concerto drowns out the characters' speech, conveying what their otherwise banal words express rather than the words themselves. And the combination of hymnlike chords, quasi-spiritual style, and women's voices in the Dvorak episode of *Paradise Road* evokes words that don't exist yet somehow ought to.

The last instance is especially suggestive because the hypothetical words are all the more powerful for being absent. Like the score, they represent an ideal object that the force, the conditions, and the exactitude of the performance can bring to life without its becoming objectified. The concerto and the Prize Song might both be said to supply a language of desire that is lacking in the world of their films. The Dvorak slow movement, performed how and where it is, represents a language of torment that may be lacking in principle.

In recent years some composers have sought ways to get the performative experience of such languages into scores that deal with extreme or limit states. In a sense, they have been rediscovering possibilities that *Paradise Road* rediscovered in the scores preserved from the prison camp. In *Different Trains* (1988), a reflection on the Holocaust, Steve Reich derives melodies for string instruments from the intonational contour of spoken phrases (heard on tape) by survivors of the era. The translation of speech-melody into music echoes the eloquence that torment has stripped from speech. But the bare speech also remains. The two forms of expression persist side by side, acknowledging by their friction the impossibility of fully comprehending the events that the music commemorates.

Composed about the same time, Kaija Saariaho's *The Grammar of Dreams* (Grammaire des rêves, 1988–89) dwells on desire, not torment, though perhaps on the torment of desire. The music, says the composer, translates the "the most important changes in the text" (collaged from poems by the surrealist Paul Eluard) into changes of color and volume: "vibratos, trills, glissandi, dynamic evolutions and certain other figures [are] used here like imaginary matrices across which the instrumental parts are 'filtered.' "

The voices of two women, a soprano and a mezzo, filter through the same matrices. Together with their instrumental alter egos—twin flutes for the higher voice, viola and cello for the lower—they take direction from a harp conceived of as a dreaming body, "a collection of restless limbs." The grammar of dreams "filters" the voices into constantly changing styles of utterance: song, speech, breath sounds, whispers, cries, singsong, pitched recitation, wordless vocalizing. Sometimes the voices share a style, sometimes not; sometimes they answer each other, sometimes not. Their dreamlike "grammar" supersedes the grammar of the text, just as the chorus of prisoners in *Paradise Road* supersedes the grammar of war. The voices flow and shimmer, ripple and dart. They fan out into a spectrum as if filtered through an acoustic prism.

Like the Dvorak and Ravel transcriptions, though in circumstances less exigent, *The Grammar of Dreams* affirms the creative power of women in a musical world still dominated by men. Dr. Praetorius would have loved it. But *The Grammar of Dreams* also follows *Paradise Road* in bringing our attention for the first time to the most universal of musical instruments, the human voice. Like the transcriptions, it gives voice, quite literally, to a domain of experience not accessible by any other means. To go a step further, neither the film's transcriptions nor Saariaho's score is content with the simple fact of voice, however expressive it may be. Both of them position, both of them catch the voice rising to peaks of longing and ecstasy. The possibility of finding those peaks, and the often surprising reasons for them, is the subject of the next chapter. There, too, we will find the transformative power of performance and the revelatory power of the fate of melody. But we will also find a new power that stems from the distinctive way that classical song combines music with words.

CHAPTER FOUR

But Not for Me

Love Song and the Heartache of Modern Life

I say of sorrow what the Englishman says of his home: my sorrow is my castle. Many consider sorrow one of life's comforts.

SØREN KIERKEGAARD, *EITHER/OR*

With a heart filled with endless love for those who scorned me, I . . . wandered far away. For many and many a year I sang songs. Whenever I tried to sing of love, it turned to pain. And again, when I tried to sing of pain, it turned to love.

FRANZ SCHUBERT, "MY DREAM"

Schubert and Kierkegaard both like to imagine themselves as failed lovers. They take a strange pleasure in it. Kierkegaard wants to live in his sorrow, which offers him all the comforts of home. Schubert finds love by singing of its loss, as a wanderer measures the comforts of home by his distance from them. The pleasure somehow comes in the distance; the loss is a kind of gift.

Put in these terms, the attitude seems perverse. Yet from Schubert and Kierkegaard's day to our own, nothing has been more normal, more familiar, or more deeply felt, at least among those who sing songs or like to hear them sung—and who doesn't?—or those who, like Schubert, write them. Schubert himself is partly responsible for this. He wrote over six hundred songs, the most famous of which gave the German art song, the Lied, the foundation of its modern tradition. That tradition flourished throughout the nineteenth century and helped foster the proliferation of popular as well as art song traditions in the twentieth. And the very core of that tradition is the strange logic of love, pain, and song that Schubert articulated in "My Dream," his sole literary effort, in part a veiled recollection of the tensions in his family life, in part the allegorical credo of a singer of songs.

What was at stake in that logic? What still is? What does it have to say about the nature of song itself, at least in the modern era? And how does it play itself out in Schubert's own songs in terms that still matter?

The German Lied was one of the best-loved art forms of the nineteenth century, but it was too closely linked to private and amateur performance to compete for prestige with the "greater forms" of symphony and sonata. For Robert Schumann, the very virtues of song, melody and immediacy, were also its limitations. In a review meant to establish Franz Schubert as "the most eminent composer since Beethoven . . . the deadly enemy of all Philistinism," Schumann expressed regret that most people in the 1840s knew Schubert only as a composer of songs. He rested his case for Schubert's preeminence on more reflective, more developmental works: a series of piano sonatas.

Schubert had virtually reinvented the art song, transforming it from a discreetly supported tune for voice to a complex dialogue between voice and piano. The achievement was not enough. Where instrumental music was universal, song was merely personal. It was also too willing to rest content with the expression of loss or longing, rather than struggle toward the affirmative resolution of difficulty, which gradually became the guiding principle of the greater forms. The problem with song was that it cultivated beauty but was indifferent to transcendence.

This indifference is itself one of the guiding principles of Schubert's two extended song cycles, *Die schöne Müllerin* and *Winterreise*, composed during the 1820s on texts by Wilhelm Müller. The amplitude of these works made them potential rivals to instrumental music in the greater forms, already exemplified above all by the music of Beethoven. The cycle format allowed song composition to achieve the integration of unity and variety, large structure and small detail, that Beethoven's instrumental works were credited with achieving. But this was a precarious achievement for the Lied, and deliberately so, since there was no custom of performing song cycles in their totality, either publicly or privately. Besides, Schubert's cycles resolutely refused the positive narrative model of instrumental music, including his own. The cycles were about suffering, about spurned love and romantic obsession and pathological brooding. And the cycles did not surmount these things but anatomized them—relentlessly. It should surprise no one that both works end not with a bang but a whimper.

Perhaps the first person to ponder these facts seriously, if only briefly, was Roland Barthes, who was fascinated by the persistent theme of abandonment in romantic song. Casting about for clues to its meaning, he lit upon the vanishing breed of the castrati, men who, in the seventeenth and eighteenth centuries, had been castrated as boys to preserve the boy's high voice but combine it with a man's lung power. Barthes observed that "it is precisely when the castrati disappear from Europe that the romantic Lied appears and immediately sheds its brightest light: the publicly castrated creature is succeeded by a complex human subject whose imaginary castration will be interiorized."

This statement is perhaps as much fable as it is history, but it is nonetheless suggestive. It certainly raises a historical question that, as Barthes says, is "perhaps not insignificant." Why does the romantically disappointed self become the ideal song protagonist in the nineteenth and twentieth centuries, passing from the Lied to popular music? Why does this splinter of subjective life become the favored image for subjective life in general, something cherished as private, authentic, and indispensable? And why—or is this the same question?—does "song" in the modern age mean, first and foremost, love song?

One possible answer is that song is, of all forms of music, the one most expressive of the performer's subjectivity. There's no mystery about why: song exalts voice, the basic vehicle of subjectivity. And of course almost everyone can sing. Unlike instrumental music, song can be reproduced in its original medium by virtually anyone who hears it. If you like a song, you can almost certainly sing it without much effort; there is a preestablished intimacy between the music and your voice, no matter who you are. So song is the place where subjectivity can most directly be performed in music. Can be and is, all the time, by spontaneous or impromptu bouts of singing. In this respect song is also to be distinguished from opera, in which the performer traditionally shows virtuosity and professionalism while expressing—and sometimes obliterating—dramatic affect.

Of course some arias have catchy tunes and some songs demand professional performance. The art song, in fact, became increasingly professionalized during the twentieth century. But in the model established by Schubert, and often simulated even by professionalized song, the singer is always potentially an amateur—potentially anyone at all, including the listener. The singer is a surrogate who sings not only *to* the listener but also *in place of* the listener. The singing is a kind of mutual ventriloquism based on the possibility of common feeling. Song is about expressive sincerity first, vocal ability second.

Given the Romantic premium on both feeling and individuality, the rise of the art song in the early nineteenth century was nearly inevitable. But that does not explain why it took the peculiar, loss-obsessed form that it did, or why that form has survived so many historical changes and is still going strong.

The tradition of nondramatic song formed around the goal of expressing poetic meaning in musical terms. This orientation derived in part from the high artistic status of the lyric poem, which was treated in Schubert's day as an oracular fragment. Even simple lyrics took on an aura of mystery from the perceived absence of the poet's living voice. Poetry was a charm against such absence. It customarily seemed to embody a vanished intention that the reader was called on to divine. Poetic expression led the reader to restore, by sensing, thoughts and feelings that would otherwise have lapsed with the voice. A key thinker of the day, Friedrich Schleiermacher, famously said that the task of the interpreter was to know the author better than he knew himself. Schleiermacher's name means "veil-maker," but his idea was that to divine a meaning was to lift a veil.

What others were discovering at the time was that music could do that as well or better than anything else. The composer's job was to raise the divination of meaning to a higher power. Song was supposed both to animate the poet's missing voice and to demonstrate the fullness of meaning in what the voice expressed. The animation came from the singer's voice as it individualized the expressive character of the melody. The demonstration came from the piano as it showed understanding by evoking the mood appropriate to the voice.

Schubert started with these ideas but did not stop with them; he discovered where they could lead. He complicated the idea of expressing meaning by refusing a pair of previously automatic assumptions. He did not necessarily treat a text's apparent meaning as its truest or most important; like Schleiermacher, he wanted above all to look behind the veil. Nor did he take it as axiomatic that the voice and the piano would interpret the poet's meaning in the same way. Both feeling and meaning were too complicated to be always of one mind about them. So Schubert cultivated a tendency to divide song into a pair of semiautonomous actions: a melodic utterance, still subject to animation by the voice, and an evocative running commentary by the piano that explores meaning rather than merely stating it. With Schubert, what the voice brings to life the accompaniment brings to light.

The result is neither a dialogue nor a synthesis, although it may have elements of both; perhaps it is best called a concurrence. In the vocabulary favored by Kierkegaard—Schubert's younger contemporary—the song simultaneously makes words more musical and music more verbal. Words, which belong to the sphere of reflection, take on the quality of sensuous and emotional immediacy proper to music, while music assumes the free intelligibility of thought.

This tendency is fluctuating, imperfect, and full of wavering boundaries, but it is nonetheless real. In the Schubert Lied, the singer forms the link between an independent text, which has a kind of voice but lacks music, and an independent accompaniment, which has plenty of music but lacks voice. The result is that the singer, who has both music and voice, becomes the embodiment of the person from whom meaning issues and to whom it applies. This person belongs to neither the poem nor the song, but rather lends itself to both without being fully determined by either. It also lends itself to the listener, whose intimacy with the singer tends to fulfill another of Schleiermacher's formulas for understanding: "Using the divinatory, one seeks to understand . . . so intimately that one transforms oneself into the other." Schubert thus carries the singing voice into the role that, as Barthes observes, the speaking voice typically plays, that of signifying the self in its totality—precisely what the virtuoso voice is unable to do.

But the self thus singled out has a distinctive character. By shifting the emphasis of song from the expression of meaning to its creation, Schubert puts the oracular text at a distinct critical remove. The song's business is not just to divine but to analyze, dramatize, and reinterpret. The self who sings is free to make its own meaning, and make meaning on its own, even at the expense of the poet's intentions, the text's integrity, or the words' accentuation. Yet the very freedom of self-invention with which this self is endowed marks it as alienated from stable, familiar sources of meaning and authority. The refusal of the poet's commanding meaning is also a loss of security. In short, the singer of the Schubert Lied is a nascent form of the modern self, ungrounded by traditional certainties. This is one reason why the protagonists of Schubert's song cycles, and of many of his individual songs, are uncomfortable or discomfiting figures: loners, the disappointed, the different, the downright strange. The self, he's telling us, is like that.

Historically, this is a self for whom the ideal of romantic love tended to substitute for broader schemes of political, social, vocational, or religious meaning, as part of an increasing general tendency to rely on private rather than public schemes of fulfillment, especially in middle-class life. One consequence is that failure in love would tend to assume metaphysical proportions for such a self. Another is that for such a self the representation of failure in love would become a compelling medium for working out the broader difficulties of modern subjectivity. And in no aesthetic medium would this be more compelling than in song, which had developed the technique to expose the self in all its emotional nakedness.

The popular ballad took over this set of topics from the Lied—topics that if anything became more urgent as the oracular status of the lyric was lost while successive waves of modernization followed each other ever more closely. Popular song, of course, avoids the fixities of the Lied: the exactly specified melody, the fully composed accompaniment, the independent text. Popular song treats melody as malleable in its essence and returns the accompaniment to a supporting role. The work of animation occurs in the singer's appropriation of the melody for his or her own voice, style, and occasion. The relation between text and voice is not primarily interpretive but topical; what the singer really interprets is the melody.

Nonetheless, both the Lied and the popular song foreground the exposure of the singer as a vulnerable being. The songs serve a common end, which is to uphold the power and authority of the wounded self, the seeker of love who has either lost or not yet found it. For all their obvious differences, the Lied, the blues, the romantic ballad, and cognate songs from many other genres have this much in common. The richer either the accompaniment in the Lied or the performativity of voice in popular song, the deeper the commitment to deprivation. If the singing subject were not wounded, why would it need a supplement?

Schubert's song cycles are seminal works for such modern love song and therefore for modern subjectivity. If they are not quite origins—too many sources flow together in this stream to admit of a single origin—they are both exhaustive paradigms and the object of uncanny repetition in a wide variety of later songs. They still matter, though, not because of their legacy, but because the command of significant detail made possible by the classical score can renew that legacy and animate it in ways that are timely as well as historical.

Die schöne Müllerin (The Pretty Miller Maid, 1823) seems like the stuff of a worst-case scenario. It traces the course of a nonexistent romance: one that, worse than failing, fails to happen in the first place. The protagonist, a journeyman miller, loves a woman who scarcely notices him; "loses" her to a rival, a hunter, without any rivalry; sinks into despair; and finally drowns himself in the brook that feeds the mill.

What's the appeal of this hopeless little story and its hapless hero?

The narrative goes well beyond the convention of the spurned lover, who is nearly always allowed to recuperate some of his injured masculinity through the force of his art. The classic instance is a slightly later song cycle, Schumann's *Dichterliebe* (A Poet's Love, 1840). Schumann's protagonist has a wider emotional range than Schubert's, including sarcasm and aggressiveness, and he begins his final song with a ringing declaration of recovered virility. The declaration proves to be equivocal, but at least the cycle has something to be equivocal about. The protagonist of Schubert's narrative not only does not recover himself but does not want to. He surrenders to the hunter cravenly, even eagerly, and rushes into a headlong embrace of supine masochism in the closing songs, which finally merge this condition into its preeminent metaphor, watery death. Not to put too fine a point on it, this protagonist is a loser. The woman he loses is more vital and more confident than he is, eager for romance where he merely yearns for it. And the figure to whom he loses her is a traditional ideal, the master of the Teutonic forest, strong, confident, irresistible to women, especially those with minds of their own.

Listeners who accept the norms that this ideal represents, no doubt too clumsily, can scarcely be expected to feel much affinity with a figure who bungles those norms even more clumsily. But they can't regard the bungler ironically without distancing themselves from the music, which has never been a plausible alternative. The lyricism of these songs is meant to be enjoyed, and it has been.

One alternative is to ignore the text and "just listen" to the music for its own sweet sake. This is probably the most common response. The result is a saving generality, a diffuse impression of beauty and youthful ardor. Even the suffering is winsome. But it is not so easy to forget—to suppress—what the songs are ostensibly about, or to ignore a narrative that takes an hour to hear. Sooner or later, the story will clamor for recognition from within the very music used to evade recognition. The cycle's appeal must at least be consistent with its handling of the story, if not with the story itself. There must be something rewarding in what the narrative does rather than what it says.

So what does it do? The basic emotional rhythm in the cycle consists of stubborn attachment followed by sudden surrender. At first the miller persists blindly in his fantasy that the miller maid returns his love, no matter how obvious she makes her indifference. (By the middle of the cycle, she is even rude about it.) Once the hunter appears and makes denial impossible, the collapse of the miller's fantasy becomes a substitute for its fulfillment, as if what really mattered were release from the tensions of uncertain hope, regardless of whether the hope is rewarded or dashed. The miller immediately gives up on everything—work, pleasure, love, and life itself. As the closing songs draw him toward the fatal brook, his surrender plays itself as an almost erotic pleasure. The cycle is "about" this letting go, the unclenching of a straining grasp, the releasing oneself from both the tyranny of facts and the pressure of desire.

The transformation can be measured by the framing of the whole. The first song identifies the miller's desire with the turning of the mill wheels, which is represented so often, and in so many ways, that the result borders on self-parody. The piano imitates the turning motion; each verse repeats both words and musical phrases to excess, as if in mechanical rotation; and this marks the song's repetition of every verse to the same music—its strophic form—as mechanistic and strange rather than as normal for a naive, folklike song.

As early as the fifth song (of twenty), the miller fantasizes about turning the wheels himself with the sheer force of his desire, if only the miller maid would recognize it. She doesn't. This song is cyclical rather than strophic; it is framed by a lumbering musical image of the turning wheels that ironically undercuts the miller's fantasy. His desire cannot turn those giant wheels; they turn him. Their rotation reveals the purely mechanical, and virtually meaningless, force of his desire.

The final song returns to the excessive strophic repetition of the first and transforms it from an image of mechanical rotation to one of organic flow. Calm in pace and rich in texture, this song is a lullaby that murmurs itself five times over with hypnotic, almost mermaidlike seductiveness. It offers sweet oblivion not just to the miller but to the listener, whoever the listener happens to be.

This song is also the one that best intimates what the cycle might have to offer the listener who is attentive to the narrative—or rather is distracted by it. *Die schöne Müllerin* may allow the listener who aspires to a more popular, more successful personality than the hapless miller's, the listener of either gender who likes the hunter or wants to be like him, to set aside the burdens of that aspiration for an hour. The cycle permits the normal, socially integrated listener to find a secret release from the strict boundaries, required aggressiveness, and performance anxiety of the normal self. Identity issues can submerge themselves without drowning. Taking pleasure in the miller's musical narrative temporarily voids the commanding force of social expectations—*Get real! Stand up for yourself! Get over it!*—that always threaten to ask for more than they can give. The music does just the opposite. It gives a pleasure that asks for nothing back.

The same problems, but not the same solutions, bedevil the next, still larger cycle, which really is a worst-case scenario. In 1826–27 Schubert set a dozen poems that Müller had published a few years earlier under the title *Die Winterreise* (The Winter Journey). The texts detail the thoughts of a wandering youth who broods obsessively over having been jilted by his sweetheart. Then, after thinking himself finished, Schubert discovered that Müller's cycle contained another dozen poems, which he promptly set. Thus doubled in size, a modest sequel to *Die schöne Müllerin* became something monumental, an encyclopedic musical study of melancholy and depression, almost a psychological case history of the kind that was just beginning to be published to great interest in the German-speaking world. Schubert shared that interest enough to take part in an experimental psychotherapy session, improvising music at the piano while a mesmerist tried to cure a patient's hysteria.

Schubert knew he had done something special in *Winterreise*. A friend, Josef von Spaun, recounts:

One day he said to me, "Come over to Schober's today, and I will sing you a cycle of ghastly songs. I am anxious to know what you will say about them. They have cost me more effort than any of my other songs." So he sang the entire *Winterreise* for us in a voice full of emotion. We were utterly dumbfounded by the mournful, gloomy tone of these songs, and Schober said he liked only one. . . . To this Schubert replied, "I like these songs more than all the rest, and you will come to like them, too." And he was right. . . . Surely there are no more beautiful German songs than these.

The reaction of Schubert's friends goes to the paradoxical core of *Winterreise*. It raises one of the oldest of aesthetic questions, one that dates back to Aristotle's *Poetics* and that greatly interested the musical aestheticians of Schubert's day. How does the representation of pain give pleasure, particularly if the pain is strong and unrelieved?

Asked of *King Lear* in the eighteenth century, the question yielded productions with a happy ending. *Winterreise* revokes the very possibility. Nor will it soften its final blow like *Die schöne Müllerin*, which laps the suicide of its protagonist in a soothing lullaby sung by the brook in which he lies drowned. *Winterreise* condemns its protagonist to life, abandoning him by a frozen pond to stare at a harbinger of his future self, an old beggar who, standing barefoot on the ice, endlessly turns the crank of a hurdy-gurdy.

How is it, then, that these unrelievedly, even pathologically bleak songs not only attract rather than repel audiences but also create an impression of beauty and strength? It is not through some tragic catharsis; on the contrary, the wanderer of the cycle plods from one state of misery to the next on a path of relentless decline. It is not through a Beethovenian appeal to human solidarity; the wanderer is so purely egocentric he can barely acknowledge the existence of other people. It is not through the process of self-development idealized in Schubert's cultural milieu; the wanderer virtually refuses to develop, whether toward resignation or resolution.

The question is itself a source of *Winterreise*'s value, and no single answer will suffice. But one possibility is that what Schubert dramatizes here is the bottomless resilience of a human psyche that, though it sees no limit to its suffering, refuses to collapse into immobility. It keeps on wandering and, more, keeps on finding creative ways to reflect upon its own condition, to turn its suffering into knowledge.

Schubert translates this resilience into music by the simplest of formal means; he puts difference where he might have put sameness. About two-thirds of the songs in *Winterreise* are strophic, but in a modified rather than a strict sense. Strict strophic songs, traditionally simple, repeat different verses to the same music. The technique assumes a stable emotional center that may change in inflection with different wordings and voicings but does not change in substance. Whatever its content, simple strophic song is soothing in form; it may be melancholy but it is virtually never traumatized. It never has to leave its emotional home. But emotion in *Winterreise* wanders without a compass. The cycle is about the loss or repudiation or impossibility of any emotional center, a trauma that paradoxically follows from being caught in the vortex of a single idea, a single person. This blend of obsession and disorientation is toxic. Applying simple strophic repetition to it would suggest a self-surrender even more extreme than the miller's and even less appealing. So Schubert does something else.

Winterreise tends to replace strophic repetition with strophic variation. The few exceptions involve compound strophes with strong internal contrasts; simple reiteration—a mainstay of *Die schöne Müllerin*—is out, except as an expression of frozen despair in the very last song, which even so varies crucially in its final strophe. Rather than strophic form, there is an impulse to strophic transformation embedded in ad hoc forms. Repetition with difference is the rule, and differently applied from song to song. This impulse also affects the third of the songs cast in circular (A B A) form, all but one of which vary the return of their first section. The net result is that we continually hear the singer engaged in acts of reinterpretation, producing or receiving signs of new feeling or insight that alter the suffering they express even if they cannot escape it. The changes involved are text-sensitive and sometimes sweeping. They are there primarily not just as means of intensification but as means of reflection. Where happiness is denied, they offer the compensations of truth. The musical action of the cycle offers to transform compulsive brooding into patient introspection.

Let one instance stand for all: "Im Dorfe" (In the Village), a song whose resonances ripple outward from the themes of this chapter to encompass those of the book.

The song is one of the three-part types that return to changed versions of their opening. In the first section, the wanderer broods on his outcast state as measured by the rattling chains and barking of the village dogs that scout his presence at night. The only accompaniment is the piano's imitation of those sounds, a pungent little phrase that occurs five times before the wanderer utters a word, as if he were listening to its jangle and snap. This restriction suggests that the mimicry is scarcely music at all, at least not yet. It is not part of a continuous expressive whole, but only a kind of primitive sound recording played in the wanderer's head.

In the B section the wanderer gives voice to his resentment of the sleeping villagers, who gain in their dreams what they miss in daily life. The piano rises here from bare mimicry to "real" music, and the change comes as an equally real relief. But the music has a tic. A single note, insistently repeated, besets the piano's effort to be expressive. Now more audible, now less, the note feels like a fragment of the external sounds that the wanderer has taken into his mind and from which he cannot get free.

That leaves the final section, the variant of the first, to settle things. Here the wanderer does not keep still and listen, as he has done before, to the rattling and barking. He sings right over them. He tries to make peace with his condition and release himself from the fantasy of being like the sleepers:

> Now bark me forth, you waking dogs,
> Let me not rest in the hour of sleep!
> I'm finished with all dreaming.
> Why should I linger among the sleepers?

This core of the wanderer's effort involves the most dramatic of the changes wrought here. A richly voiced chord progression on the piano, something with no counterpart earlier in the song, accompanies the final question. This happens twice, the second time with even greater fullness. The nonmusic of the rattling and barking gives way to a fundamental musical sound, chords gathered into harmony, leading to a cadence.

This harmony is metaphorical as well as literal, a harmony within the psyche; the chords move in synchrony with the wanderer's words and thoughts, in contrast to the external noises they interrupt. Shutting out the sounds from outside, including the jabbing note of the middle section, the chords create an imaginary place where the wanderer belongs, though he cannot call it home: an interior village for one, which goes wherever he does. They do so with a striking major-key serenity that rises to a certain majesty, at odds with the words being uttered, which could well be spoken in tones of resentment or contempt. Those are the very emotions the wanderer is refusing, and refusing by means of the music he calls into being around him. Here, perhaps for the only time in the song, the music represents what he feels, not an assault on his feelings.

The details, readily heard, enrich these impressions. The rattling and barking always sound softly in the first section, but at the start of the third their volume rises in a steady crescendo as the wanderer's despair reaches its peak. The sounds seem literally to be getting to him, getting into his head. But then the volume suddenly drops again, as if he had, so to speak, started to stop listening, so that what *we* hear is the way a sound sounds when it's unheeded. This is the sound of a mind in the act of changing, coming to terms with itself at whatever cost in lonely resignation. When the wanderer dismisses the sleepers, he makes his own crescendos, embracing his despair by using it as a means of self-understanding. The result is to curtail the musical mimicry: to call off the dogs. The painful sounds dissolve like the dregs of a bad dream. They seem to disintegrate, losing the little snap that has given them bite, dispelled by the meshing of chords and vocal line that records the decision to wander both further onward and further inward.

The fate of melody thus permits the wanderer to endure his own fate better and to move on undestroyed, if not undismayed. Every change in the music matters, and that it matters is what makes the music subjectively vital. For this companionless man, his suffering is indeed his castle. He may not love his fate, but as the music tells us, and him, he need not hate it. Like many later examples, the torch song lights the singer's path.

But we need something more from this song. Nowadays it is easy enough to praise the discovery of inner strength or truth and to ground the sense of self there. Doing so is even old-fashioned (not to say quaint) in a world of media saturation and continuous virtuality. But in Schubert's world this habit of mind was still in its infancy, especially if we think of the interior as psychological, and hence secular, rather than spiritual. The music does not invoke a preexisting formula for subjectivity. Instead it helps to create a formula that spanned almost two centuries and still operates today, if only as an ideal, an alternative, a fantasy rather than a fully supported institution. And the music adds an insight that is unexhausted and severe—a hard truth, indeed, if we believe it: that the inner refuge can only moderate (and never cure) the suffering that has led to it, that subjective depth is accessible only on condition of real or, more likely, metaphorical homelessness, isolation, abjection. Subjective depth is a wound; the self is the scar that covers it. The love unavailable to the wanderer might have made him happier, but it would not have made him deeper. It might even have left him shallow.

The therapeutic project dramatized by songs like this one is basic to European Romanticism and to the broader experience of modern life of which Romanticism was a part. It defines a historically new mode of heroism, the presence of which in *Winterreise* is consoling and reassuring not in spite of the music's somberness but because of it. At stake in this discovery was not just something that music could express but something that music could do. Song became an instrument of self-acceptance, especially with regard to the fraught issues of dependency, vulnerability, and regret—never absent, of course, even from happy love—and other music would follow its example. The tradition of self-transformation built up around the idea of Beethoven would find the partner and rival without which neither tradition could flourish.

For Kierkegaard, the ear was not a passive organ but the active "instrument" of deep human contact. It is by lending an ear that the sense of hearing draws the inner being expressed by the voice of another person into a listener's own world. Ideally, the result is empathy and understanding rather than mere appropriation, though there is no guarantee of that. Either way, Schubert's songs are depictions of a similar process. The inspired poet remains the paramount source of song texts, but the figure of the poet in Schubert's songs is an unabashed musical invention, a kind of fictional character animated by the song. The animation arises in part from text-setting and performance, but first and foremost it arises in the relationship between the voice and the piano. This is the primary *dramatic* medium of the relationship between poetic utterance and its musical revoicing that also diffuses itself throughout the song.

In the first instance, above all in Schubert's "pathological" song cycles, this is also the relationship between suffering and reflective awareness. In *Die schöne Müllerin* the utterances of the suffering protagonist are often naive or deluded; the supplement of the piano is required to make the truth apparent. In *Winterreise* there is no such division of labor; the voice probes its wounds side by side with the piano, even in excess of it. Reflection on suffering has become a suffering that is itself fully reflective. But it has not thereby become redemptive, except insofar as persistence is redemption. It has just become modern.

Between them, Schubert's song cycles can be heard to advance two of modernity's defining agendas. In *Die schöne Müllerin*, it is the perspectivism that contemplates how the self can make a world out of its own defects. In *Winterreise*, it is the psychopathology that composes the self out of intricate layers of deception, secrecy, obsessiveness, memory, and fantasy. *Die schöne Müllerin* dignifies the embrace of suffering; *Winterreise*, more rigorous in its modernism, turns the embrace of suffering into a heroic adventure.

Most men, wrote Shelley, "are cradled into poetry by wrong, / They learn in suffering what they teach in song." What the Schubert song cycles suggest is that song reveals, or perhaps actually produces, a power over meaning that compensates for loss of power over life. Suffering dies in song to be reborn as meaning. Unlike Kierkegaard, Schubert apparently did not regard this power of song over suffering as primarily an aesthetic phenomenon. "What is a poet?" Kierkegaard asked through the persona of an aesthete. "An unhappy man," went the answer, "who in his heart harbors a deep anguish, but whose lips are so fashioned that the moans and cries which pass over them are transformed into ravishing music." Kierkegaard's poet is less a human being than a mechanical instrument, an automaton for the production of a music that "ravishes" the listener, who is thus rendered nearly as prostrate as the poet. By contrast, the poetic voices of Schubert's song cycles may be passive in the face of their pain, but the music that absorbs them is relentlessly active in its interpretation. The majority of the songs in both the completed cycles are deliberate efforts to make sense of the suffering they express. To do that is also to prevent the relationship between suffering and art from becoming merely mechanical or addictive.

In this regard Schubert anticipates Nietzsche, who says that human beings are willing to endure any amount of suffering as long as it is meaningful. The problem is that meaning cannot come, in modern times, from preestablished systems of belief, be they religious, political, or ideological. If you can't do without such things, if you can't maintain some distance from them, this music is not for you. These are all elements conspicuously missing from Schubert's song cycles. They are missing, by and large, from the world of absorbing particulars—of simple scenes, sharp sensations, and strong desires—that the Lied tends to dwell in and not to look beyond. Meaning has to come from art, from song, which must evolve from suffering without merely reproducing it, yet without falsifying or prettifying it either.

But where does art get the meaning that it gives? Nietzsche had several famous answers: from Dionysian frenzy, from vital energy, from the will to power. But it's not clear whether even he thought these terms were anything more than metaphors for something that could not easily be identified in conceptual terms or easily be found if it existed at all. The absence of such a grand source is basic to the experience of modernity. And so, too, is the gradual acceptance that the true source is less than grand, less than metaphysical, less than universal. Meaning, we've learned to say, is socially constructed. It sounds so easy, and is surely so true, that many of us don't even notice the burden it brings.

Meaning, the subtext runs, is *nothing but* socially constructed. All meaning is nothing but that. The wider implications of this principle are spelled out in an eloquent statement by Pierre Bourdieu: "Doomed to death, that end which cannot be taken as an end, man is a being without reason for being. It is society, and society alone, which dispenses, to different degrees, the justifications and reasons for existing; it is society which produces . . . the acts and agents that are judged to be 'important.'"

. The desire not to accept this idea is also basic to the experience of modernity. And one way not to accept it, even if you happen to believe it, is to hear someone sing a song of loss or longing.

Preferably to see the singer, too, and perhaps even to sing along or sing before or after, but above all to hear, to listen. That's what song has been under the condition of modernity: a refusal to accept that the loss of a grand source is the loss of meaning, a refusal to accept social authority as a second-rate metaphysics. The ability of the suffering individual to feel and sustain desire, especially when to do so is irrational or self-destructive, is meaning enough. By giving that subjective ability voice, and such a voice that we cannot help but listen, song accomplishes its work, which is to prevent our ever reaching Bourdieu's position. "I like these songs more than all the rest," said Schubert, "and you will come to like them, too." And as Spaun said, he was right.

In a sense, then, the meaning that song gives, that art gives, has no identifiable source. Song after Schubert claims this as its strength. The meaning has to come from nowhere, like the hurdy-gurdy man at the end of *Winterreise*. The hurdy-gurdy man is not only a figure of desperation but also a figure of perseverance: a figure for what will not be annihilated, even if condemned to walk on ice, and what will not, at any cost, stop making music, even of the barest, scrappiest kind. If he has to sing with the voice of a machine, he will. The hurdy-gurdy man defines singing itself as heroism. And though he represents an extreme to which song rarely needs to go, the model he represents tends not only to underwrite the art song after Schubert but also to support a central tradition of modern popular song— that vast tradition based, so pleasurably for so many, on thwarted desire, defeated romance, and lost love.

But let's not forget the hurdy-gurdy, or rather the piano that so faithfully imitates it, gathering up the bare bones of sound that the song needs to stay alive. The voice in song may live on loss, but in classical song it needs its partner's help.

Looking back on this chapter, we might notice a strange omission. When we think of song, what comes to mind is obviously voice; songs are for singing. Yet classical song, as we've seen, involves a fully scored accompaniment, in the first instance for piano. The piano has figured in our discussion, to be sure, but it has not been much considered in its own right. As I said, the omission is strange, even though the mesmerizing quality of the singing voice makes it understandable. The next chapter will turn the tables. That it can do so is a historical fact of great importance, and one that reveals a major source of classical music's continued power.

One question that haunts most classical song is whether the piano will also "sing." The piano often aspires to the condition of voice; expressive playing is often designated by the term *cantabile*, songlike. This vocal aspiration is a key element in the piano's role as the central instrument in the classical tradition, a role that developed as the tradition took its distinctive shape in the nineteenth century. The piano is the partner of the voice, not only in song, but across a whole musical culture. One result is that, even today, the sound of the piano is so familiar, so basic, that the sheer strangeness of its expressive life is obscured. What does it mean to say that an instrument can sing? What does it mean of the piano in particular, which not only is unconnected to the mouth and lips and throat but is a hulking machine, bigger than the person who plays it? These questions are about to loom large.

CHAPTER FIVE

The Ghost in the Machine

Keyboard Rhapsodies

The ghost in the machine, or rather the machine with a ghost in it, is us: you and me. The philosopher Gilbert Ryle coined the phrase to show the absurdity of conceiving the mind and the body as utterly separate entities. Ryle may not have been aware that experimenters with artificial life had been trying to make machines with ghosts (like Intel) inside since the middle of the eighteenth century and that the combination fascinated rather than bothered most of them. A good case can be made that one of these machines was the concert piano.

The design of the instrument is richly suggestive of this. The sound, full of lifelike expression, comes from a large heavy box whose mysterious interior is obscured by a jutting lid. Like the person as conceived by this era, the grand piano houses an interior that one may peer at but not see. It is both a mystery of spirit and a technical puzzle. The frame on which the strings are stretched is called the harp, connoting the instrument of inspired, age-old song, the vibrating tones of which are produced in close proximity to the body of the player who sings while playing; but the devices that make the sound are called the hammers, connoting technology, industry, machinery, force, the whole apparatus of modern enterprise.

The nineteenth century could hardly have found a better musical emblem. The piano is the instrument par excellence for the expression of feeling, sensibility, mood, the inner life, but it is also a large, unwieldy machine. The expressive side of the instrument is warm, vital, and imbued with spirit; the machinic side is impersonal, automaton-like, as remote from spirit as the advance of modernity often seemed to be. Much of the piano music composed in the nineteenth and twentieth centuries— which is to say, most of the piano repertoire—is about some version of this paradox.

The terms of the paradox, of course, do not form a simple opposition and sometimes do not seem opposed at all. The piano, harp and hammer, the machine with a ghost inside, embodies both magic and engineering. As harp it is a machine that the player's hands (and feet; the pedal is critical) lift into organic life so that its machinic character disappears. As hammer, the piano exposes the mechanics of dream; its machinic element exposes as artifice a feeling, a world of feeling, that constantly reinstates itself as natural, true, sincere, timeless.

What do we mean when we say that music expresses states of mind, the attitudes of a specific type of self? How do we experience this expression? What does classical music contribute to it? And why does classical piano music play a special role?

These are questions for the ghost, not the machine. But the two cannot be kept apart for very long (they like each other too much). Exploring the one will uncover hints about the other and gradually lead us back to their long marriage.

One answer is suggested by my own experience as an amateur pianist whose great pleasure is to play pieces too hard for the very modest ability I can bring to them. It may seem strange at first to take playing as a model for listening, though of course anyone who plays is listening at the same time. But with the piano this makes good sense, even for people who have never touched a key. No other instrument binds playing and listening more closely.

So: there I am at the keyboard, knowing that the music I'm looking at is too hard for me. The fact that I cannot effortlessly meet the demands of this music enhances my awareness of what those demands are, of how the piece is put together, where it's going, the logic behind it all, the actions my hands must execute to realize a portion of it. Doing all this is extraordinarily absorbing; it can make one forget everything else. And at some point, when things go well, or well enough, the experience of performing creates the very powerful illusion of inhabiting another mind.

Listen hard, and the same thing may just happen—or almost. The experience of performance seems built into piano music in a special way. Like a voice, the instrument transforms certain basic acoustic realities into something utterly personal, something singular. It does so by its endless shadings of color and volume and its control over the decay of sound. The piano's unique capabilities—to span many octaves, to modulate from a whisper to a roar, to translate touch into sound, to accompany itself in textures of three, four, even five instrumental voices, and to do all this at the bidding of a single person—make performance itself uniquely audible. We always hear the pianist in the piano, the ghost in the machine.

This is as true of recorded performances as it is of live ones. In other words, it does not depend on our seeing the pianist at all. In the era of sound recording, we hear piano performance far more often than we see it. Yet this shift in the usual conditions of our experience does not negate the piano's performative character but only displaces it to an imaginary scene. This is still the scene of listening, but it is a scene transformed by the addition of other senses in virtual form. With the piano we see with our ears and hear, kinesthetically, with our hands. Some part of us hovers over an imaginary keyboard. This is still the scene of listening, but it is, so to speak, lit up from within.

The history of the piano might be written as the gradual discovery and development of its ability to create an intimate space in which playing and listening meet, touch, part, and meet again. This ability may be one reason for its central and iconic place in the culture of classical music. It allows the piano to become a microcosm for the whole enterprise.

The other mind I inhabit in the space around the piano has no simple or fixed identity. It sometimes feels like what one imagines the composer to have been, in part an authorial figure, in part a historical one. This impression thrives on the equation of style and person, our ability to recognize the person from even just a few bars of music. Nineteenth-century observers sometimes described the result as uncanny, almost supernatural, as if the piano were part of a séance.

But this is not quite right. The person in question is one that the composer too must impersonate. The mind that hovers behind any given piece is a fiction created by the piece. It belongs to the composer the way a dramatist's or novelist's characters belong to their authors: we know what a Shakespearean or a Dickensian or Wagnerian or Faulknerian character is like. So this mind I inhabit is a role, a personified attitude and style, but just because it is recognizably so it also touches ground in the historical reality of its author, who inflects it without possessing it. The mind is thus both real and fictitious. In this it is only a particularly vivid version of any other mind in the only way I can access other minds, including those in my own collection of past and future selves. This blend of the singular and the social, the individual and the type, is the source of the charisma that envelops the soloist at the keyboard, either myself or one with whose solitary address to the keys I identify. The pianist is the emblematic figure in whom the crossover from one self to another occurs.

It is important in this context that what the pianist plays is not improvised. There must be a score; it must be performed note for note; the pianist and composer must go one on one. (The one-on-one requirement gradually changed the standard of the pianist's artistry from the ability to play one's own music, as Chopin generally did, to the ability to play music by others: to channel other minds.) It is the act of such performance that carries out the transcription of thought and feeling from one mind to another. Although popular music is also deeply invested in questions of identity and identification, it is not invested in just this way. Popular song, in particular, tends to fuse the charismatic persona of the performer with the substance of the music performed; the music is designed to be fulfilled when this happens. But classical performance keeps these things separate, and nowhere more so than in the meeting of minds at the piano, which, strange though it sounds to say so, enhances the charisma of the performer precisely because it is just what I called it, a meeting, in which the music maintains a substance that nothing and no one can subsume.

This substance has long since become one of the theme songs of this book. The full effect of subjectivity depends on the experience of the music as a "work" in the classical sense of an enduring embodiment of lived experience. In playing through a score, I participate in the work process. I track and enact the fate of melody. Because I do, the realization of that lived sensation of another mind is unusually vivid. For fullness and immediacy, it has virtually no rivals in other media.

The closest parallel probably comes in the theater, including musical theater. Its source is the prescribed speech with which an actor "creates" a character in a play against the background of myriad other creations that will utter the same words to different ends. The actor shapes the language with speech melody as an opera singer, in a similar case, does with actual melody. But the pianist's subjective aura exceeds the actor's or the singer's. The subjectivity evoked at the keyboard feels like reality because its fictional quality is only implicit; there is no story to set it at a distance. And the pianist, unlike most actors or opera singers, is "on" all the time. Even more than a stage performance, my performance at the piano becomes an impersonation that at times can make even the impersonator forget who he is.

It is impossible to say whether this meeting, this merging, of minds is a real or a virtual event. The boundaries between the real and the virtual break down during this experience; that's part of the point. The music tangibly occupies the zone where subjectivity itself comes into being. It distills the way that persons, like dramatic characters, become animate through performance and create their varied personae through performance. Distills this: captures it as energy, sensation, intuition, direction.

Anyone who voices a melody knows something of what this is like. All it takes is the act of singing or humming to become the subject whose inner state the melody expresses. It can even happen subvocally. Melody alone is a means for moods to circulate. But the pianist playing through a classical score, following the fate of melody in all its twists and turns, becomes something—or someone—else. The pianist's own persona, no matter how highly colored in itself, becomes a vehicle for the persona whose career the music imagines. Song can provide a revealing contrast, and this time it does not matter whether the song is popular or classical. A singer, any singer, embodies a persona found in the song, or, more often, found through the song. But the pianist performing a classical score embodies nothing. The performance is itself the embodiment. All the pianist does is perform the music: a statement that should be regarded as remarkable, not as obvious.

In calling for this imaginative self-extension, the piano music only does with singular directness what classical music does in general. It binds the fate of the self to the fate of melody, to music that must work and play, struggle and adventure, to become what it is. It joins a heightened expression of subjectivity with a heightened lucidity about the subjectivity expressed. It fosters a consciousness of self that is not an alienating self-consciousness.

This combination seems to have impressed many nineteenth-century listeners as a direct revelation of the life of feeling. They spoke unabashedly about it in those terms. They developed habits of attention and response that fostered this impression and that trained them to emulate the kinds of self they felt summoned to meet in the music. They fiercely contested the music's subjective character and the best and worse ways to fulfill it. Obviously too much history has intervened for us to reproduce these practices today. But the emotional trust so many of us place so readily in music of all kinds shows their continuing influence, as well as the continued vitality of the music that nourished them. Our times may be telling us that subjectivity itself is old-fashioned, but perhaps that just makes us hunger for it more. The signs of the times suggest as much. Classical music can help fill our emotional needs; all we have to do is let it.

When we listen to such music without performing it, the subjectivity involved finds a new medium. It turns from practice to fantasy, from action to imagination. But not from activity to passivity: as a listener I retain a strong sense of agency, just as I incorporate a high degree of receptivity as a performer. It is just that my efforts are imaginary, and imaginative; I grasp the music with my mind, not my hands. With orchestral or chamber music, the tendency is to feel enveloped or suffused by the sound; I apprehend the music as if from inside it, even as I feel it inside me. With piano music, given its special nature, my listening tends to incorporate a layer of virtual performance. The sounds gravitate to the bodily dispositions needed to make them, which I can feel as well as hear. The pianist becomes my surrogate—at least as long as I like what I hear.

The experiential difference between playing and listening is hard to describe. It's like seeing the same landscape by sunlight and moonlight. In listening the telepathic illusion of performance arises like a metaphor; it gives the listener a sense of being on the inside of a lived subjectivity but of visiting only, not of dwelling there. Yet the effect still feels more immediate than anything available through either words or images. The music opens up the zone in which one subjectivity cannot clearly be separated from another.

This zone is more than merely illusory. It is basic to our most far-reaching encounters with one another. Music is one of the media in which it is imagined and also one of the means by which it is created. What occurs in the zone is imaginary, but the zone and its effects are real. Classical music not only opens this zone of intermingling but also constantly enlarges and deepens it, maps it and explores it in intricate and surprising detail, finds in it not only a destination but also a point of departure. By the early years of the nineteenth century, the piano had become the nerve center of this enterprise: its model, its symbol, its primary means of dissemination.

Which brings us back to the machine. The piano decisively changed the relationship between art and technology, not least by making it impossible to ignore. Not until the invention of cinema would another device have such an impact. Unlike the fabled "cinematic apparatus," though, the pianistic apparatus does not stay out of sight; it doesn't reveal itself only as a faintly glittering beam of light gliding across the darkness. The piano looms large. Just how do you get those ghosts in (or out) of it?

The general answer for the nineteenth century was: by how you handle the thing—literally. Practically speaking, this tended to involve choosing between a pair of complementary attitudes, though of course the two could mix. The first was the attitude of heroic virtuosity, personified by the early career of Franz Liszt, who overawed audiences all over Europe during the 1830s and 1840s. The point here is to master the instrument, to wring subjectivity from mechanism—as the poet Heinrich Heine famously said, to make the keys bleed. The other attitude was of intimacy with the instrument, personified with equal celebrity by Chopin. The idea here is to make the instrument an extension of one's own body, to coax the spirit out of it, transcend mechanism, make it disappear, make the instrument sing. The first of these models was strongly visual, the second withdrawn from visuality. The first emphasized technical prowess at the possible expense of sincerity (Liszt the genius was also Liszt the showman); the second emphasized expressive richness at the possible expense of power and breadth (some said that Chopin played too softly, others that he had no need to play louder).

The two models prevailed into the early twentieth century, when they were joined by a third: the possibility of identification with the machine, of taking the machine as substitute spirit. The Italian poet Filippo Marinetti gave voice to this idea in his infamous "Manifesto of Futurism" in 1909—with the help of musical metaphors: "We will sing of the multicolored, polyphonic tides of revolution in the modern capitals; we will sing of the vibrant nightly fervor of arsenals and shipyards blazing with violent electric moons; greedy railway stations that devour smoke-plumed serpents; factories hung on the clouds by the crooked line of their smoke . . . and the sleek flight of planes whose propellers chatter in the wind like banners." In his poem *Owl's Clover* (1935), Wallace Stevens satirized this conception by imagining a "Concerto for Airplane and Pianoforte" played from a bandstand. But ten years earlier George Antheil's *Ballet mechanique* had in fact included airplane propellers along with several pianos in its scoring.

Ravel and Prokofiev both wrote toccatas for piano (literally touch-pieces, originally a Baroque form) that clatter and rattle in this spirit. Ravel's suggests a cheerful automaton with occasional dreams of coming alive, Prokofiev's a dynamo that chugs and churns regardless of anything. Prokofiev made the interplay of mechanism, lyricism, and automatism a primary issue in his piano music, which constantly juggles all three alternatives. At the other extreme stands Messiaen, defiantly wringing spirit out of matter in his works like his massive collection, *Twenty Gazes on the Infant Jesus*. Messiaen literally thinks of music as color and seeks to shape its rhythms and sonorities into moments of "bedazzlement" in which both the listener and the music touch the divine in their contact with each other.

Underlying all the possibilities of spirit and mechanism at the piano was what might be called the romance of tone: the pure sound of a vibrating string. It was common during much of the nineteenth century to think of tone as incipient music, both in itself and as an analogue to the sensitive vibration of human nerves. Tone felt like the vibratory presence of life and sensibility.

The technology of the nineteenth-century piano encouraged composers to make tone in this sense the protagonist of the drama of inner life. The instrument's sensitivity allows tone to sound as an extension of the performer's touch. The pedal allows tones to blend beyond the span of the hand and makes the duration of tone a basic expressive issue. Unlike wind or string instruments, the piano cannot keep tone from fading; it can only slow the fade. The pedal poses the tones it prolongs against the concurrent movement of their inevitable decay. The music inspired by this effect tends to hold it up for contemplation, to reflect on its uneasy balance of mechanism and sensation, to contrast it to the quickly decaying sounds of unpedaled tones when the fingers leave the keys. Such music draws on the romance of tone to give a special quality of both ecstasy and melancholy to the sound of its instrument.

It is in this context that a new type of piece comes to the fore: the Romantic character piece. This was an independent composition for piano that typically evoked a particular mood or scene; most examples lasted anywhere from just under a minute to just over ten. The character piece tended to displace the multimovement sonata, already thoroughly colonized by Beethoven, as the piano's cutting-edge form. Nineteenth-century sonatas, Chopin's and Schumann's most prominently, often assimilate the traits and logic of the character piece. (Schumann said that the name "Sonata" for the work containing Chopin's famous Funeral March was just a pretext for the composer's gathering together of "four of his wildest children.") The difference, though, was perhaps less one of form than of attitude. The character piece is designed to be yielding to the pianist's touch. The activity of performing is composed into its melodies and textures so that the animation of the notes is to be heard, and, by the player, felt, not as a realization of the music, abstractly conceived, but as a part of the music itself.

The more this happened, the more the subjective animation of tone became associated with its simulation on a musical machine whose versatility rivaled that of the voice. The association fostered a desire to explore as wide a range of feelings, moods, and states of mind as possible. The piano seemed to call for its own subculture of feeling; character pieces poured forth to answer the call. As works of art, these pieces offered themselves as real if fragmentary expressions of sensibility, as samples of the true self. As products of technology and technique, they acted as so many masks, personae, lyrical fictions. Between these alternatives lay a protean give-and-take of expression and construction, the acoustic equivalent of a multifaceted glimmering.

In keeping with this, character pieces were typically published in groups, often in large collections. These compilations rarely form organized wholes, though in the era of sound recording their pieces are often played together, as also in modern concerts. Originally they would have been for the player to leaf through and try, in any order, such pieces as he or she liked or could master. The point of the collections—of rhapsodies, intermezzos, nocturnes, etudes, preludes, ballades, fantasies, and the like—is to spread out the unlimited possibilities of feeling and reflection, passion and memory, available at the piano keyboard.

The variety suggests a deliberate jumble. It addresses a player or listener in whom a limitless number of impulses and attitudes overlap, contradict, and combine with each other. Such a person acts not as a whole being but as the sometimes unwilling or unwitting bearer of these interlacing agencies; the self is not a person but a population. This hall-of-mirrors effect is associated with piano collections ranging over nearly two centuries from Chopin and Schumann through Debussy to Ligeti. Mechanism and lyricism, or the technical and the organic, are by no means the only questions this music raises, but they are both pervasive and highly adaptable.

Some of these questions concern the ghost in the machine directly: How can feeling survive, and even thrive on, its mechanical production? Sometimes they ask about meanings and consequences: What are the psychological or social implications of living in a world of feeling defined by this very question, in which performance as expression is always in negotiation with performance as technique or performance as display?

Chopin is a key figure for the first question, Schumann for the second.

Chopin's music, virtually all of it for piano solo, circulates mainly among three expressive resources: songlike (cantabile) melody supported by the pedal, evocative of the supple, florid style found in the operas of his friend Vincenzo Bellini; dance rhythm, expressed in his many waltzes and Polish dances (polonaises and mazurkas); and touch, conveyed by the wide palette of textures and effects uniquely the piano's own: scales, runs, and arpeggios bound together by the pedal, octaves, passages in parallel intervals, blurs and buzzes of sound, streams of chords, and so on. Any of these things can tip into either animation or mechanism at a moment's notice. The pedal can be magical or contrived, the dance rhythms lithe or rigid; the exercise of touch can be just that, an exercise, a show of dexterity, or it can translate speed, strength, and the manner of striking the keys into the external substance of feeling.

Chopin typically sets either a song or a dance impulse, or more rarely both, in interplay with and against the discipline and expressive force of touch. Voice or the body swayed to music confronts the power of the hands to strike, tap, flourish, caress, and manipulate, and sometimes (being quicker than the eye) to confound. To some extent, the outcome depends on performance—as we know. The piano is an acoustic stage; the role of the pianist in general is to bring the music to life. Or rather, to be *heard* bringing it to life by infusing the instrument's mechanism with sensibility. But Chopin and others sometimes compose this challenge right into the music.

Nowhere does Chopin do this more ambitiously than in the big, sweeping Polonaise-Fantasy of 1846. This piece draws both song and dance impulses (delicate arias, dashing polonaises) into a texture of unparalleled complexity and energy that pushes both the player and the instrument to their limits. This music wants its melodies to transcend themselves and doesn't mind if they destroy themselves to do it. It invites us to hear a musical mechanism literally trying to translate itself into spirit, no matter the cost, and all the more powerfully for never quite succeeding. The piece comes to a long, tumultuous conclusion after returning to its introduction: lurching chords that give way to keyboard-spanning arpeggios woven together by the pedal, the most basic, most elemental form by which the piano makes its mechanism a principle of animation.

As an expression of vital or lyrical impulse, voice tends to take priority over the body for Chopin. Many of his dance-based pieces are rich in cantabile melody, and a play or opposition between song and dance impulses, independent of the question of mechanism, occurs frequently. It is quite remarkable how often phantom voices figure in Chopin's music, with imitations of chant, chorus, and ballad recitation as well as solo song. Chopin is known to have approved when a friend, the soprano and composer Pauline Viardot, made and performed song arrangements of four of his mazurkas. And Chopin's own reputation for expressive sincerity, especially when he was the performer, was linked to a sense of hearing the piano sing in his voice.

This point is worth dwelling on a moment longer. Voice is the first among equals in Chopin's expressive triad of voice, dance, and touch, almost as if for him, anticipating many others, the voice is richer and fuller in its simulated pianistic form than in the throat of a real person. There is a real rivalry between the pianist and the singer as the paramount classical performer. Perhaps this is because playing the piano, for both the player and the audience, and even on recordings, is the most direct means of experiencing classical music's great distinctive features: the life of the score in performance, the accumulation of meaning through luminous detail, and the realization of the fate of melody. All of these things are literally in the pianist's hands.

Although the vocal impulse is everywhere in Chopin, its presence is most concentrated in his nocturnes. These are instrumental evocations of a serenade, a song to be sung at night, in which the quasi-vocal melody combines with accompaniment textures reminiscent of a guitar or lute. Strange as it may seem, the imitation assumes a greater degree of evocative power than the music it imitates. The piano seeks not to simulate the serenade but to imagine it. The nocturne is not an expression of feeling from the depths of night but an expression of the nocturnal depth within the one who feels. This psychologizing or spiritualizing of the musical texture manifests itself especially through the pedal, which merges the mimic sound of the serenader's instrument into the rich vibratory aura that subtends expressive voice.

Chopin also took the nocturne as a testing ground for the fate of melody, often constructing three- or multipart forms in which the internal episodes are highly disruptive, challenging the melody to adapt or resist in response. Many nocturnes of this type make the initial songlike expression of sensibility seem in retrospect like artifice; what first seemed supple threatens to stiffen up. When it returns after a touch-based middle section has run an impassioned course, often a frenzied and percussive course, the opening section has to decide what to do about it. Will it repeat itself or vary, and how much? Will it expand or contract? How will it end? In the course of deciding, the return may also have to reckon with ambiguities and shifts of perspective in both the middle section and its own original version. Feeling in this music is constantly on the move.

The possible outcomes are endless; anything can happen. Among other things, the opening can reinvent itself by returning to break its own spell, evolving into a texture and melody beyond its original reach (Nocturne no. 7 in C# Minor). Or the return can absorb the agitation of the middle section and subordinate it to the flight of song (Nocturne in no. 13 in C Minor). Or, on the contrary, the returning music can distance itself from the turmoil or messiness of too much passion and embrace its own artifice as a refuge. It can come trailing ornamental flourishes that, in excess of any heard the first time, break up the vocal quality of the melody into purely pianistic textures (Nocturne no. 5 in F# Minor). Or, again, the return can dissipate into a pedaled haze (Nocturne no. 4 in F Major) or kindle into a brilliant flare of color (Nocturne no. 3 in B Major). Either choice dissolves mechanism itself into an elemental acoustic reality and evokes the metaphor of vibratory presence as pure feeling. Or the return can just crumble under the strain (Nocturne no. 15 in F Minor).

The Nocturne no. 3 (1833) combines and reshuffles many of these features in exemplary ways. The opening melody is lilting, half song, half dance. Prone to flights of both mechanism and feeling, it drapes itself in sudden swirls of ornament but also evolves and envelops a rich, more warmly lyrical song. The middle section takes wing by dissolving a fragment of the lilting theme into a seething mass of hammer-blows and high-velocity figures, as if to expose something false or hollow in the opening, a touch of puppetry in its mixture of attitudes. But the opening melody has inner resources, and it uses them. It toughens up its rhythmic contour, pares itself down to a terse, heroic form, cuts across the seething texture, and refuses to die. When the opening returns, it returns *from* the tumultuous center, not from beyond it. And the returning melody knows just what it has to do—or do without. It does without its songlike expansion. Called on to prove itself, it stands on its own, curtails its ornamental impulse without giving up on it entirely, and sings. This lyrical self-enrichment ends with a rise, arialike, to a single consummating high note and then a new discovery, a phrase that reflectively lingers out the close. After that the music flames up into the coloristic climax and dies away in a quiet shower of sparks.

Schumann wrote exclusively for the solo piano during the 1830s before branching out to other genres. Unlike Chopin, he rarely suggests an antagonism between the inward and the mechanical; instead, he casts inwardness as a reservoir of spirit that energetic, virtuosic music can tap. When the two types communicate with each other, the inward assures sincerity and passion to the energetic and the pull of the energetic keeps the inward from too much self-absorption. This productive relationship becomes a model for individual creativity and social vitality, unhampered by timidity or needless constraint. Perhaps for this reason, Schumann, unlike Chopin, never questions an expression of sensibility or inwardness; all the risk is channeled to the outside.

This is the underlying idea of Schumann's collection *Davidsbündler*, composed in 1837. The title signals one of the leitmotifs of this book. *Davidsbündler* is best translated simply as *The League of David* or *The Davidites*, a mythical band of artists ranged against the middlebrow middle class designated as Philistines, people who demand a safe, comfortable beauty and reject artistic adventure. Schumann's original title was *Davidsbündlertänze*, Davidite Dances—an ironic concession to the Philistines, since none of the music is dancelike. He described the up-tempo numbers as "death dances, St. Vitus dances, dances of the Graces and of goblins." This is music to jangle the nerves of the world's Professor Elwells.

The figure of David combines two streams of imagery: David the warrior, slayer of Goliath, a biblical Jack the Giant Killer who brings his antagonist down with an unconventional weapon, a slingshot, that immediately translates the force of his body into the force of his will; and David the psalmist, a biblical Apollo who combines praise of God the Creator with the highest powers of human creativity. Ideally speaking, the character piece for piano is Davidite as part of its very definition, though as Schumann well knew (and resented, given the sales figures), many composers cranked out piano music for the Philistines, who favored it precisely (or so he thought) because it reassured them that they were in the know.

The eighteen pieces of *Davidsbündler* avoid the kind of ambiguity that fascinated Chopin. They wholeheartedly embrace either inner feeling or outer display. Schumann famously associated these qualities with a pair of artistic personae, the guiding spirits of his piano music: Eusebius, the poetic introvert, and Florestan, the passionate extrovert. The two personalities may either take over separate pieces or occupy different sections within the same piece. Both are excessive by Philistine standards; in *Davidsbündler* they represent the socially transforming power of art and imagination. The energy behind that power belongs to Florestan, the genius to Eusebius; the idea of the collection is to give Florestan free rein while grounding his passion in Eusebius's depth. The opening piece does just that in miniature. The collection as a whole does it at large.

The second piece plays a special role in this process. Like most of the reflective music in the cycle, it is playable by pianists of modest skill, unlike the demonstrative pieces, which require virtuosity; the difference marks the ever-present danger that the two personae will separate rather than mesh. Schumann marks this piece "Innig" (inward). Its purpose is not just to express inwardness but to portray the process of turning inward, of delving into one's own secret self.

"Innig" (which I will co-opt as a title), continuously runs together its bass, its inner voices, and its melody into a flowing single line, yet it does so while keeping each voice clear in itself. The melody would be skeletal, literally superficial, without the addition of the inner voices. The hands have to traverse these in a fluid, sensitive motion connecting the bass to the treble with the help of the pedal. The idea is to produce a sense of supple absorption that not only is both audible and tactile, but, for the player, ripples throughout the whole body; inwardness is engaged at every level. It sounds with particular acuity in the expressive dissonance that the pedal and the melodic fluency of the hands render a source of overflowing feeling rather than a source of tension or unrest. The almost hypnotic motion of the hands, as audible as it is tactile and visual, continuously turns the incipience of unrest into sensibility and pleasure.

This balance of forces is the goal of the piece as well as its animating principle. "Innig" hesitates throughout over whether its key is major or minor. When at last it decides for the minor it confirms its declared inwardness. Inwardness is vulnerable.

Keeping faith with it requires the willing embrace of poignancy that informs the whole piece.

The same hesitation arches over the collection as a whole, which reaches the same conclusion but raises the stakes. The seventeenth piece ends with the unprepared return of "Innig," complete—or so it seems at first. The repetition becomes a recapitulation as "Innig" returns to its own opening only to find itself moving faster and faster, and in a crescendo, whereas originally it had quietly kept its pace. This upsurge of passion propels the music into a tumultuous B-minor coda that comes to a strong, dark, decisive end. But the element of display in this passage is too external, too theatrical, to end with. The return of "Innig" has closed a large circle, but the coda forces a supplement. The collection needs an extra at the end to match the beginning, the first piece, which the circle excludes.

This extra reverts to the pristine key of C major. It is a slow, static piece, all inward, serenely withdrawn from all formalizing and rationalizing. Schumann originally gave it an inscription, later removed: "Quite superfluously, Eusebius added the following, while great bliss radiated from his eyes." The addition is superfluous because it, too, lies outside the circle of melodic and tonal return, but its expressive alliance with great bliss makes clear that this formal superfluity is an emotional necessity. In a very different context, Messiaen would end his *Quartet for the End of Time* in a similar way, with an ecstasy made possible by the logic of melodic return that it transcends.

Schumann liked to emphasize the individuality stamped on Chopin's music, the immediate recognizability of his authorial hand or pianistic voice: "Chopin will soon be unable to write anything without people crying out at the seventh or eighth bar, 'That's by him, all right!'" "In every piece we find, in his own pearly handwriting, 'This is by Frédéric Chopin.'" The same distinctness belongs to Schumann himself, although he could—and did—do a drop-dead perfect Chopin impersonation. He put one in his collection *Carnaval*, much to Chopin's annoyance.

This individuality is fundamental to the aesthetic of the character piece. At stake here is not just the familiar idea of a Romanticism that departs from traditional culture by placing a high value on individuality. The character piece, or more exactly the pianistic enterprise epitomized by it, contributes to a change in the very nature of individuality. It helps to fashion a new concept of the person and takes its place among the practices that give training in how to become such a person—and to keep on doing it, because there is no end to the process. These practices form the building blocks of an aesthetically informed, non-Philistine culture. Their aim, and the culture's aim, is not to initiate people into a traditional community by showing them how to be. It is, instead, to establish the conditions under which people can fashion themselves into singular selves, selves understood as singularities. This aim requires a continual negotiation in which what each person becomes weighs equally with what the community asks a person to be. The result is the paradox of a self united and divided like the two hands at the keyboard, each one constantly acting for itself and the other alike. But since the aim is obviously utopian, it may be realized more fully at the keyboard than anywhere else.

This paradox is also a particular concern of another variety of piano music, the Romantic piano concerto. Commercial and practical considerations aside, the difference between the concerto and the character piece lies in their approach to self-fashioning. The concerto engages in processes of interpretation and intimacy in dialogue with the orchestra. The character piece is more directly subjective, more like a monologue or soliloquy.

In Schumann's Concerto (1841–45), the orchestra appoints the oboe to present the sweet-sad opening theme with the sense of pastoral distance, remoteness in both time and place, familiarly associated with the instrument. The piano applies this idea to itself, rendering the theme inward and contemporary, enriching it with harmonic color and eventually surrounding it with supple, rippling figures that span the keyboard. The relationship between the piano and the melody approaches the erotic as the piano caresses the melody, forming an intimacy with it that is romantic in the amatory sense. Something similar happens in the slow movement of Tchaikovsky's First Piano Concerto during a series of dialogues between the oboe and piano. The oboe intones either of two folklike themes, nostalgic and distinctly Russian; the piano turns each into a more cosmopolitan, reflective utterance. The movement includes similar exchanges with the flute and two solo cellos; Schumann's does the same with the clarinet.

Such concertos project the self in constant motion between its inner world, which it turns outward, and the outer world, which it draws inward. Character pieces represent this process in fragments; they take chips of it as moments, moods, singular events. These pieces seek the goals and take the risks that occupy Schumann in *Davidsbündler:* to render introspection transparent at the risk of introversion; to display energy and virtuosity at the risk of theatricality. The aim is to validate the breadth of the second in the depth of the first.

The inwardness of solo piano music does not represent solipsism or a retreat from the world. It proposes an alternative means of social connection: a step in the growth of the mind, in a personal history, in the education of the feelings or the combined education of fantasy and intellect that Schumann would have known as *Bildung* (formation; but the term is untranslatable). The external display of piano music does not represent mere theatricality. It proposes a turning outward of inwardly authenticated feelings and convictions. Or so the music likes to imagine. So it invites us to imagine. Of course the inwardness could become solipsism and virtuosity could become empty display. It happened, and happens, all the time. Or rather, *not* all the time, which is really the point. What's remarkable is how often something else happens.

The dangers go with the idea, but they are not the idea itself. The piano rises to prominence in part just because its keys are the keys to the kingdom of modern identity, its medium the telepathic-sympathetic embodiment of feeling and the ability to give that feeling a technological basis. The result is a state of mind or being that we would now call virtual and that earlier generations happily took (meaning chose to take, willed to take) for real. The piano does not so much express feeling as devise models of feeling that both player and listener can follow. The instrument's mechanical qualities—we've come upon them often: the range of pitch and volume, the sensitivity to touch, the power of self-accompaniment, the pedal mechanism—coalesce to produce the very qualities we most often ascribe to feeling, and to produce them with greater clarity than feeling itself often possesses. The feelings thus made available change with changing times, but the underlying process is remarkably consistent. (It really does seem to come from the character—the spirit and/or the mechanism—of the instrument itself: witness jazz piano, which discovered its own version in the twentieth century.) The piano draws an acoustic graph of what we ask feeling to be and to do, questions and demands that are changing again today in ways we are still struggling to comprehend.

The result is both ambiguous and ambivalent, and all the better for it. The lyric impulse is constantly haunted by the suspicion of artifice, of mechanism; more and more it risks looking fake or insipid. Its greatest task and triumph is to revalidate itself (or die trying). This becomes increasingly so as modernity advances, as lyricism comes to stand for tradition and mechanism for modern novelty and energy—and sometimes for modern violence. The mutual relation, interference, and promotion of these alternatives, present from the start, increasingly become an explicit part of what piano music, especially the character piece, is "about."

The key modern idea of alienation readily takes over as the context of this process, and often as its content too. The antagonism of personal aspiration and social demand becomes common coin, more notable for its role as a structuring principle than for any possible resolution. It's just what modern experience looks like, feels like. Reconciliation and alienation become each other's open antagonists and secret partners. The modern can never escape the longings of and longing for the Romantic past it disavows. In a world of matter, spirit lives on as fiction, illusion, dream, diminished but not destroyed by the irony that shadows it and the mechanism that both denies it and mimics it.

In the articulation of this drama as a social practice, an art practice, and a presence in everyday life, the piano and its music played a primary role. In many respects they are still playing it. We talk of playing the piano, but when we grow absorbed in this music, we are the instrument on which the piano plays.

Even music with motoric rhythms, say those toccatas by Ravel and Prokofiev, music intoxicated by the pianistic machine, all hammer and no harp, is deeply ambivalent. It remains so today, when mechanism is no longer the sign of modernity but is fully assimilated into the texture of a life that has already fully absorbed its digital successor. On the one hand, the music is robotic, dehumanized. On the other it expresses the energy that survives and continues, an essentially comic energy, represented as organic in its traditional form, that here assumes the cool, hard shell of its modern metamorphosis. The organic—the warm, soft, wet energy of life—now shifts toward the lyrical, which in its traditional form had understood itself precisely as a transcendence of such life toward its sublimation in spirit. This music shows how stubbornly the past (the spirit of the past, the past as spirit) lives on: how, as the historian of science Bruno Latour expresses it, we have never been modern.

Ravel and Prokofiev have more to say about these tendencies. The composers' toccatas, of course, embody only one side of their musical personalities. Each of them felt his allegiance divided between the ghost and the machine. Ravel was intrigued and amused by this; Prokofiev was conflicted.

Ravel often wrote music for piano that he later orchestrated. Perhaps the best-known example is "Le Tombeau de Couperin" (Couperin's Tomb, or, more idiomatically, Homage to Couperin, 1917–19); the title suggests a tribute to the eighteenth-century French composer François Couperin, but in fact Ravel wrote the music as a tribute to friends and comrades who had died on the Western Front. In this and other instances, the orchestral versions soften the edges of the pianistic originals and give them a vivacity with no shadows. Ideally, a listener should always hear one version against another, equally willing to be pleased by artifice or illusion. Ravel's famous orchestration of Modest Musorgsky's *Pictures at an Exhibition* goes a step further, as if to animate a work that would otherwise be lifeless—a series of character pieces for piano with a reputation for being "unpianistic." Although not originally for piano, *Bolero* is also worth mentioning in this connection. The work consists of many repetitions of the same music in a long crescendo. The repetition is mechanical, the music sensuous; the combination is unstable, as the catastrophic climax noted in chapter 3 reveals. In this connection, too, it is interesting that the vocal transcription featured in *Paradise Road* stops before the impression of mechanism can gear up. As a piece for voice—the ideal other side of the piano—*Bolero* is all sensuousness and rhythmic impulse, which is one reason it serves so effectively as an act of tacit rebellion against the women's captors.

Prokofiev's music is often described in terms of a tug-of-war between motoric modernism and Romantic lyricism, and a similar pattern may be found in the work of more hard-edged modernists such as Bartok and even Schoenberg. This conflict is epitomized by the opening of Prokofiev's Third Piano Concerto (1921), where the first sound we hear is an unaccompanied clarinet caressing a plaintive melody. The strings take the melody up and quickly turn it into a soaring Romantic statement—then change their minds and launch into rushing scales. The piano takes this as its cue and enters the fray with bright percussive clatter. Modernist skepticism defines itself against a Romantic sensibility that it cannot help longing for, however covertly, while reanimations of Romantic sensibility are haunted by the modernist suspicion that they have lost all credibility, that they represent only a wishful disavowal of the hard facts of modern life. Hard-boiled music claims truth at the possible price of becoming dehumanization; soft-boiled music claims human warmth at the possible price of being sentimental delusion. But it is a mistake to think this quarrel can ever be settled. The music is less the expression of a quest for resolution or reconciliation than a depiction of what life is like under the conditions of this perplexity, which is the historically determined condition of modernity.

The capacity of classical piano music to sustain this argument with itself may make it especially valuable in an age that uses music relentlessly to reinforce monolithic commercial and dramatic messages, a culture that often treats music of all kinds as generic "product" meant more to be labeled than heard. It is revealing to pair off pieces by Chopin or Schumann with twentieth-century character pieces so as to hear some of the lines along which the argument develops. Such pairings can show different facets of the interplay of lyricism and mechanism that operates in both the nineteenth and twentieth centuries as a cultural symptom, but that also represents the discovery of new human possibilities, with rewards and deficits not available under other circumstances, to selves formed under a different star.

Between 1985 and 1995 György Ligeti composed two collections of concert etudes ("studies") plus a first installment on a third. Chopin cultivated the type: piano music that simultaneously aims to explore a technical problem and to create a fully realized expressive world in the meeting of one player and one instrument. For Ligeti, such music comes directly from an intimacy with the piano in which mechanism continually translates itself into feeling and vice versa. He describes a process that begins with a touch: "I lay my ten fingers on the keyboard and imagine music." Almost instantly "the anatomical reality of [the] hands and the configuration of the piano keyboard" combine to transform the music he has imagined. The musical idea undergoes a series of metamorphoses, both in the grip of impersonal forces—he speaks of a feedback loop, a mill wheel, meshing gears—and in the grasp of the hand that must feel its way to the music. "For a piece to be well-suited to the piano," Ligeti adds, "tactile concepts are almost as important as acoustic ones; so I call for support upon the four great composers who thought *pianistically:* Scarlatti, Chopin, Schumann, and Debussy. A Chopinesque melodic twist or accompaniment figure is not just heard; it is also felt as a tactile shape, as a succession of muscular exertions. A well-formed piano work produces physical pleasure."

Ligeti's etudes draw inspiration from a scientific as well as pianistic grasp of the problems of animation and mechanism. The music shows the influence of chaos theory and fractal geometry, which demonstrate how the repetition and overlapping of simple patterns produce effects of great complexity, even disorder, from which a higher order paradoxically emerges: the whorls of a shell, the behavior of clouds, the flow of liquids. Ligeti (who finds the same effect in the rhythms of African music) tries to emulate what he calls "[the] wonderful combination of order and disorder which in turn merge together producing a sense of order on the highest level." The etudes evolve through ever-changing recombinations of simple scales and rhythmic patterns, following an impersonal, even implacable logic that makes demands of extreme virtuosity on the pianist.

Yet sooner or later—and often sooner—the play of mechanism becomes the vivid evocation of a feeling or perception, as suggested by such titles as "Vertigo," "In Suspense," "Interlacing." "Rainbow," and "Autumn in Warsaw." The textures may also incorporate purely subjective elements—those Chopinesque melodic twists—that intrude on the naturalistic process from without or erupt from within. The music absorbs the logic of the character piece and goes it one better. Matter and spirit are so intimate, so interlocked, in these etudes that the distinction between the two repeatedly disappears.

"Vertigo" is exemplary. It consists of overlapping chromatic scales, pattering away at top speed, always descending, the entries growing progressively closer. Like Bernard Hermann's score for Alfred Hitchcock's film *Vertigo* (whether by coincidence or allusion I can't say), the etude seems to stagger in circles; vertigo is not what it expresses but what it induces. Yet from amid the dizzying cascade of notes, melodic lines episodically emerge, some faint and fleeting within the busy texture, some cutting across it sharply; some finish with a dramatic or sensuous chord, in a piece where chords are otherwise lacking. A look at the score will not show these melodies; the page seems to consist of nothing but a stream of eighth notes. The melodies can only be heard. Many of the etudes cultivate a similar illusion, as Ligeti calls it, though it is not quite clear whether the illusion is the melody's presence in the performance or its absence from the score. Either way, expressive subjectivity returns at, or as, the core of the vertiginous clockwork. The etude invokes the melodic twists less as pianistic surrogates for voice than as manifestations of voice in its true, inward form.

Chopin wrote a similar piece; it is one of his most famous. The last of the "wild children" in his Second Sonata, it follows the Funeral March with a minute and a half of dark, surly octaves moving at breakneck pace. Except for the last sound we hear, a single, utterly arbitrary chord, there is nothing else. By nineteenth-century standards the movement lacks melody, harmony, and rhythm; Schumann found it riveting but also said it was not music. Yet as in "Vertigo," what is not there is—there. Combined with the speed of the playing, the resonance of the instrument lets harmonies sound, ghostly melodies emerge and float above the vortex, rhythmic profiles take fleeting shape. The feeling is spectral, not robust as in "Vertigo." Where Ligeti suggests the birth of subjectivity within the organized chaos of natural process, Chopin confronts us with the uncanny residue of a subjectivity that refuses to die. Perhaps for that reason, his piece is more elusive than "Vertigo," harder to follow, perhaps, than any of Ligeti's etudes.

"Infinite Column," the climactic last etude in Ligeti's second book, is certainly not hard to follow but almost impossible to play; in case of emergency, a version of it exists for player piano. The title refers to a thirty-foot-high public sculpture by Constantin Brancusi consisting of pyramids alternately stacked base to base and tip to tip. Like the column, and in direct contrast to its counterpart in "Vertigo," the music continuously ascends. Each hand draws two streamers of chromatic scales upward at top speed, with overlapping entries and constant crossing of hands. As the piece proceeds, the ascents reach higher and higher peaks until the music recedes into the extreme upper reaches of the keyboard. The result suggests a fountain or geyser erupting at high pressure as much as it does a column, which is part of the point: the music suspends the difference between liquidity and solidity as much as it does the difference between spirit and matter.

"Infinite Column" is at one level a metaphor of gazing upward in both a physical and a spiritual sense. Like Brancusi's column the music integrates virtuoso mechanical technique with a sense of wonder or astonishment that soars beyond its mechanical basis without for a moment forgetting it. The etude "studies" not what the gaze sees but how the gazer feels as vision ascends and soars. The ecstatic closing moments, echoing the close of the first etude, "Disorder," suggests the age-old trope of divine radiance: the music acts like a gaze blinded by light as the rising streamers concentrate in a blur, a nimbus, of high-treble, no-bass brilliance sounding at top volume. Chopin's third nocturne finds a similar, if less absolute, apotheosis but holds it less firmly. Unlike Ligeti's etude, the nocturne cannot end on high; the etude could end nowhere else. It concludes with a consummating *ping!*—one can hear both the note and the hammer striking the very short string—of a single note in the piano's highest register: the point at which the gaze vanishes into the infinite.

The seventh piece in Schumann's *Davidsbündler* traces the same ascending arc with lyrical excitement rather than frenzy, but with a driving inner tension created by the persistent use of arpeggios under the melody. The melodic pace is moderate, marked "Not Fast," but since the left hand has to arpeggiate the accompanying chords, it must speed from note to note to squeeze them all in on time. The left hand must move quickly in order *not* to hurry. The chords involved tend to increase in breadth until they exceed the hand's span, a tendency that itself increases as one group of chords—there are six of them—succeeds another. The first section divides unevenly into clusters of two and four groups, both repeated, the short half more restrained, the long half progressively less so.

Each group follows the same basic pattern: the melody climbs to a peak atop an unbroken succession of arpeggiated chords, then crumbles away as the arpeggios lapse. The climbs begin with small steps but tend increasingly to continue with wide leaps and to reach ever higher peaks as the first section proceeds. A feeling of effort predominates, as if the melody were trying to wrest itself from the grip of some dark retarding force and always failing. But on the last attempt it succeeds: the melody rises through an extended series of leaps, the peak lies in the top register of the keyboard, and there is no crumbling away. Instead, after the moment of brilliant color that marks the final arrival, the music discovers for the first time what key it is in. Its breakthrough has made the discovery possible.

The middle section makes the same discovery in its own last measure, but without the corresponding sense of excitement or release. For better and worse, this section is effortless, a study in acquiescence, even passivity. It is lyrical and attractive enough, and Schumann gives it the room to make its case. But it seems to wear out its welcome. Its lack of aspiration begins to sound timid; it induces impatience. When the opening section returns, the effect is like flinging a window open in an airless room.

The return is highly concentrated, an affirmation of essentials. The music skips its tentative beginnings and brings back its ardent second half in a single, decisive, unclouded repetition. It rebuilds its own image of an all-but-infinite column of arpeggios with newfound certainty and speed. When it ends, exactly as it had before, its true goal appears not as the quiet, down-to-earth chord that completes its final cadence but as the brilliant *ping!* that starts the cadence and that would, if it could, be an end unto itself at the column's inconceivable top

The high-altitude conclusions of both "Infinite Column" and the seventh number of *Davidsbündler* push toward one of the outer limits of music; Ligeti's "Blocked Keys" pushes toward another. The hand-crossing that helps produce the endless agitation of "Infinite Column" here tends toward stasis and silence. As one hand sweeps back and forth over the keyboard, the other perches motionless, holding down a group of keys. The moving hand does nothing to avoid these blocked keys; increasingly it seems to seek them out, or to be drawn to them by some fascination or attraction. The silence that results is unlike any produced by observing a rest; it has a distinctive mechanical quality, a tooled precision, that intensifies as the music continues. At first the silences form little pinpricks in the sound; then they widen to rips, eyelets, holes. The wider they become, the more their silence is filled with the faint patter of the fingers on the keys, forming a kind of phantom music, neither breaking the silence nor observing it. By the end, the music's texture has reversed itself: a sound stippled by silences has become a silence stippled by sounds. There remains only an unanswerable question: Is what we come to hear a collapse of music into its broken mechanism or the production of a higher music in which the mechanism gives the sounds of the moving hand a kind of acoustic afterlife?

Chopin asks a similar question in his Nocturne no. 9 in B Major. Here, as in the third nocturne, we first hear a light lyric theme, then a warmer counterpart. This time, though, there is no middle section, just a large, two-part melodic arc, each half of which has a varied repetition. Each segment in this pattern contains a sudden silence that disrupts the flow of melody: not a pause but a fissure, like a crack in a china cup. The length of the pause is up to the pianist; in each case the music resumes after the striking of a single note deep in the bass. But the breaks make no sense—if they do at all—until the surprising conclusion.

The piece concludes with what sounds like a sketch for the middle section that never was. The passage is patchy and impatient and prone to violence. It yokes together four disjunctive phrases, the second an intensified form of the first, the others quite disparate. The effect is more random than improvisatory, but the phrases do have something in common. Each of them ends with an exposed tone (a note or octave) the sound of which is abruptly blocked by one or more short, hard, loud chords— "stingers," as film composers would later call the type. The result the first three times is a dead silence, carefully notated to last longer than the earlier cracks in the melodic surface. Then, as in the Ligeti, a reversal occurs that reveals what is truly at stake as the cracks widen into gaps. The fourth and last phrase tries to hold out against the inevitable stingers, but its success—and it does succeed—leaves it grasping at nothing. The music ends with the pianist holding a deep octave *through* the last pair of stingers, so that they first block and then reveal its slowly dying sound. The actual finish is the fade-out of the octave, which is held without pedal. It is a finish that exposes what the pedal so often conceals, the abyss of silence waiting to consume the music the moment the hand lets go.

Just how annihilating this ending seems is partly up to the performer and the listener, and for that matter the instrument and the performance space. But it has certainly become impossible to forget that the earlier vivacity and lyricism have a mechanical basis. Whatever illusion remains, it can't be naive. Chopin is in some ways more "modern" than Ligeti in the degree of negation. His naked exposure of the pedal as mechanism goes unmitigated, where in Ligeti the silence of the blocked keys may—just may—hold out the alternative of a reverse perspective, breaking through to a realm of spirit more real in its silence than the one it replaces.

Of course there are no certainties about any of this; that is part of its meaning. But Ligeti does retain the possibilities that Chopin dismisses. It is Chopin, the Romantic, not Ligeti, the modernist, who has a streak of real nihilism in him, something usually suppressed by lyric aspiration and the refinement that never departs even his most turbulent writing—qualities kept in place as if by a stern will. "Blocked Keys" expands Chopin's silence to create a phantasmal counterpoint between the sounds emitted and the sounds blocked. The blocked sounds at first seem to be a phantom of silence, but eventually they become a virtual substance. As the balance of power gradually tips in favor of blockage, the semianimate voice of the instrument fades into the mechanism of silence—but perhaps not entirely. Perhaps some remnant of tone still haunts the silence with a semblance of life.

In a sense the whole modern history of the classical piano hangs on that "perhaps." "Blocked Keys" is both a condensed image of that history and a venture to its outer limits. The close of this etude is thus where this chapter should close too, almost its appointed destination. The moment of suspension between sound and silence, the animate and the inanimate, may perhaps serve equally well to epitomize this chapter and prefigure the next, which asks how classical music might sound when moments of crisis threaten to silence it. The answer will also involve blocked keys, in the sense that it exceeds the reach of the keyboard; it demands the symphonic. But "Blocked Keys" exceeds the reach of the keyboard, too, and the results perhaps show why an answer is possible: just perhaps. So perhaps, indeed, the voice of the instrument does not entirely fade. The fragments remain articulate, hang on, protest. They are still spirited, these fragments. They throw their voice into the phantom's *tap, tap, tap* to make it, perhaps, the lively movement of the ghost in the machine.

CHAPTER SIX

Crisis and Memory

The Music of Lost Time

One of the oldest ideas about music is that it can ease a troubled mind. The Roman poet Horace said so in four words that four words can translate: *Minuentur atrae carmine curae*, "Song will diminish gloom." This healing potential is traditionally associated with a style of sweet tranquillity, often vaguely hymnlike, often in the vein of a reverie. Liszt, for example, wrote a series of "Consolations" for piano that are not only in this vein but, unlike most of his music, easy to play, as if he wanted to make them widely available as the inevitable occasions demanded.

But the healing force of music is not limited to overt consolation, or to consolation at all. Some music heals by lamenting, some by inspiring hope. Classical music can do that too, and console just as well as other kinds, but its healing power lies above all in its capacity for drama. It heals by finding a logic to deal with darkness and by giving that logic expression in the fate of melody. The result may be the liberating energy celebrated in chapter 3, which works against forms of darkness both great and small; or it may be the stoic passion of the love song tradition considered in chapter 4, which embraces meaning when experience fails; or it may be the quarrel of animation and technology, the ghost and the machine of chapter 5, from which the piano builds up its expansive subculture of feeling, a homeland of feeling from which one cannot be exiled. Healing, of course, is only one of the many concerns touched on in these chapters. Yet it remains something we often ask of music, which does not disappoint us in reply. *Minuentur atrae carmine curae.*

But what role, what power, does all or any of this have at a moment of real historical crisis? Why, to return to the question posed in chapter 1, was it so important to invoke music in the aftermath of September 11? When symphony orchestras put on special concerts during those first dark days, the music did seem to diminish gloom. How was this possible? And how, more pointedly, was it possible with classical music, music remote in both form and spirit from much of today's world?

This question has no quick, easy answer. But it does have a modern history that may suggest an answer. I'd like to follow a significant thread in that history from past to present, through both high and popular culture, in search of one remedy for troubled minds, in troubled times.

1808 was a very bad year for the empire of Austria. The best you could say for it is that it was slightly better than the years just before and after. Since 1805 Austria and its allies had been pummeled by Napoleon's armies; in 1808 neither Austria nor Prussia could claim to be a great power. This was not simply a matter of being defeated on the battlefield. The defeats were epic in scope, obviously landmarks in military history; Austerlitz and Jena were humiliations of the highest order. In 1809, defeat would come to Austria again at the battle of Wagram: Vienna would be occupied, territory ceded, and indemnities paid to France. 1808 was a battered breathing space between one disaster and another.

It was also one of the great years in musical history. In 1808 Beethoven wrote only four major works, but they are quite a group. Two of them, the piano trios published as opus 70, are well known to lovers of chamber music; they are definitive works in their genre. The other two are definitive works in Western music generally, pieces that virtually everyone has encountered at one time or another, on soundtracks if nowhere else. In 1808, Beethoven completed his Fifth Symphony and composed his Sixth, the *Pastoral*. The two were actually premiered together in one monster concert at the end of the year.

Both symphonies embody responses to the crisis in the air about them. They do so both in their own right and in the way they complement each other as a matched pair. These responses are not necessarily direct, even in the militant Fifth Symphony. Beethoven, it's true, did say at that time that he would like to emulate the Roman Camillus "who drove the wicked Gauls out of Rome." But he realized that good symphonies make poor calls to arms; you can't have an intricate four-movement "Marseillaise." So the Fifth doesn't try to stir up the Austrians against the French. Instead, it tries to stir up the energies of a utopian liberalism from which any listener can take inspiration. That's one reason the music has traveled so well. The Fifth identifies the utopian release of energy with passage through adversity and a willingness to be aggressive in the service of an ideal. It's almost an essay in Roman virtue, still a standard-setter in 1808.

The other compositions of that year make similar moves to a level of principle or myth that applies to the troubled present without specifically referring to it. The trios pose questions about the precariousness of ordinary life; the symphonies ask about the impact of the extraordinary. The way to grasp any of this music as a response to crisis is to ask how the crisis atmosphere may have contributed to a sense of timeliness. This is the sense that just these pieces in particular were what the times demanded, music that would seem fresh and imaginative and pertinent under the special circumstances of its creation.

I want to explore that sense and to bring out its wider implications for both Beethoven's era and our own. Doing so will involve more than asking how the music traces imaginary pathways from crisis to recovery. It will also involve the recognition that finding such pathways depends on the building up of cultural memory, the cultivation of a sense of living tradition. My focus will be on the symphonies, the more consequential of the year's compositions. And here the lion's share of attention will go to the *Pastoral*. This, the less powerful, less heaven-storming, and far less angry of the two symphonies is the one that holds the key to the whole problem that Beethoven began to address in 1808, the problem of how to write music for a time of crisis.

On the surface, the Fifth and Sixth Symphonies are stark opposites. The Fifth was and still is one of the most violent, conflict-ridden pieces ever composed. The *Pastoral*, except for the portrayal of a thunderstorm that precedes its finale, is almost conflict-free. Its music is bathed in a benign luminous energy that overspreads the work's forty-minute span. According to an old bromide, Beethoven's odd-numbered symphonies are dramatic and progressive where the even-numbered ones are relaxed and conservative. At first blush that seems true enough here.

On reflection, though, these symphonic contraries prove to tell much the same story. The differences between them are more in the telling than in the tale. Sooner or later, both speak of a severe disruption, a sublime shock, that must be overcome. The Fifth Symphony conquers it; the *Pastoral* leaves it behind. Both works lead to a phase of crisis, which both surmount through an incremental transition from disruption to overcoming. These transitions intertwine separate musical movements by blurring the borders between them, a departure from normal symphonic protocol in 1808. The goal in each case is to forge a triumphant conclusion, a finale brimming with pleasure and freedom. The finale is meant to feel true, even inevitable, because it has so clearly evolved by logical-organic steps from the transition.

This alliance between logical-organic form and some sort of upward-bound narrative is certainly familiar. It was one of the nineteenth century's most powerful essays in cultural mythmaking, and it has been resilient enough to survive successive waves of twentieth-century irony, critique, and disillusionment. It has perhaps been especially important for classical music, whether as an ideal, a model, or an icon to be shattered. With Beethoven as a paradigm, it has been one of the prime organizing features of the symphonic tradition. But its roots and its uses in times of crisis have not been widely recognized. Its wider impact, together with the full range of its cultural associations, has been underappreciated even by those who value it the most. My aim here is to start filling in the blanks, which by the start of the twenty-first century have begun to make the music itself look blank.

The first step is to review the dramatic outlines of the Fifth and Sixth Symphonies, familiar as the works may be, against the silent background of historical events. The background will break its silence rarely if at all, but its presence will bring out the details by which the music sounds out the possibilities of crisis and recovery, memory and hope.

It's generally acknowledged that the Fifth Symphony is an effort to get from turmoil in C minor to triumph in C major, an imperative reflected in each of its four movements. The trouble is that the music can't seem to find a C major it can keep. Achieved after much violence in the first movement, the major collapses into a still more violent minor. Apparently triumphant C-major fanfares in the slow movement *harrumph!* too much and fade into nothing. The third movement begins in a harsh C minor and consigns C major to its middle section. This is a grotesque gambol led by the double basses, a gleeful, heavy-footed mockery of itself. What follows is a less friendly mockery as the first section returns in hoarse whispers like a disturbing thought that won't go away.

Only at the beginning of the finale, after a long transitional passage, does a secure C major seem to emerge. Its emergence comes in response to an endless series of timpani strokes on C as the transition very slowly wends its way forward. The strokes continue unabated to the brink of a C-major cadence while the orchestral sonority evolves from dark to bright. The music clears up as its sense of direction clarifies and we find we can hear what's coming, also more clearly with every stroke: this music will diminish gloom. Softly but surely, it will beat down C minor along the way. "Give me the major," the beating drum seems to be saying, "*I want the major.*" When C major does finally burst out, Beethoven underlines its triumph by adding trombones, piccolo, and contrabassoons to his orchestra for the first time; the outburst pushes the acoustic envelope as far as possible in height, depth, and volume. But even this roaring affirmation turns out to be illusory. The music will eventually spin out of control, unable to separate exuberance from violence. The transition that led to it will have to come back again, in tatters but in full, to set things right. Only at the very end are we really in the clear.

The narrative of the *Pastoral* Symphony is far simpler than this, as befits its genre. The subtitles of the five movements basically tell the whole story: 1. Awakening of Cheerful Feelings on Arriving in the Country. 2. Scene by the Brook. 3. Merry Gathering of the Country Folk. 4. Thunderstorm; Tempest. 5. Shepherd's Song; Happy, Thankful Feelings after the Storm.

Nothing to it, you might say, and you might be right—except for the storm. Like many a thunderstorm, this episode doesn't last all that long, but its impact is enormous. The storm music is the bomb in the garden. It is as violent as anything in the Fifth Symphony and represents a force more implacable than anything in that ostensibly more heroic work. In its own day this movement had the impact of state-of-the-art cinematic special effects. According to Hector Berlioz, writing in 1834, "it is no longer an orchestra that one hears, it is no longer music, but rather the tumultuous voice of the heavenly torrents blended with the uproar of the earthly ones, with the furious claps of thunder, with the crashing of uprooted trees, with the gusts of an exterminating wind, with the frightened cries of men and the lowing of the herd. This is terrifying, it makes one shudder, the illusion is complete." In a famous—and literal—stroke of genius, Beethoven waits until the storm music before he uses the timpani, which disappear again afterwards. As Berlioz's remarks suggest, the sudden outburst of percussion could be quite unnerving, as if one had never heard a drum before.

The storm music is the fulcrum of the *Pastoral* Symphony. Its intrusion is what gives meaning and narrative direction to the whole. The way its force is quelled goes to the heart of the cultural myth that this symphony shares with the Fifth. This myth has shown remarkable powers to console or inspire in times of trouble. It is time to look more closely at it, especially as the *Pastoral* tells the story.

The *Pastoral* Symphony embodies a type of nostalgia that has tended to surface whenever the forces of modernity and urban life have seemed to threaten the continuities of traditional culture. This is not, though, a simple cause-and-effect relationship. The unity of traditional culture may or may not have existed in fact, but it certainly exists as fiction in the cultures that have supposedly lost it. A constant give-and-take with such fictions is one of the sources of social reality. Pastoral in particular is the fiction that mitigates the sense of cultural loss by channeling it into nostalgia, a pleasure tinged with the pathos of distance in time or space. Both the mood and the narrative of the *Pastoral* Symphony have served as important modern models for evoking this nostalgia. The prestige of the work, the culturally potent fact that it's a symphony by Beethoven, has served to make the nostalgia legitimate.

This legitimizing role comes out intriguingly in some of the responses to Walt Disney's *Fantasia* (1940), which illustrates selections of classical music with cartoon narratives. Most people seem to agree that the animation in this movie does justice to the music, with one fairly common exception. The exception is the *Pastoral* Symphony. The point would have been lost on Walt Disney himself, who was so delighted with this episode that he reportedly said it would "*make* Beethoven." The consensus has been that it only manages to unmake the *Pastoral*.

On the surface this is a matter of the kitschy mythological images devised by Disney's animators. Ignoring all the standard traditions for depicting pastoral, *Fantasia* populates the wrong locale—Mount Olympus—with cutesy miniaturized figures in a vaguely Art Deco style. Bad taste meets the cultural prestige of Beethoven and crumples under its weight. So say the objectors who are allergic to centaurettes, and they're probably right. But a sharper pang of dissatisfaction may underlie this sense of offended taste. The disparity felt between the music and the imagery suggests that the world pictured in the movie is not pastoral enough. It is not lost enough, not worthy enough of being regretted. The symphony not only helps define a modern form of pastoral nostalgia but also sets a standard for it.

Part of that standard is the principle that the pastoral world should be evoked with no overt sense of loss or ironic distance. The remote appears as if it were near. The element of nostalgia comes entirely from its context, the silent background I spoke of earlier. The *Pastoral* Symphony was first heard under the shadow of Napoleonic power and the concurrent sense of impending cultural and political collapse. How *would* it sound under the circumstances, even if the circumstances were not explicitly referred to?

The silent background has guided the way music from the symphony has been used over the years to evoke a better world under the shadow of loss. Here are three examples, all involving the first movement, the touchstone of the symphony's pastoral spirit.

To start, a public spectacle. The *Pastoral* Symphony entered popular culture early, especially in England, where it was a great favorite in the nineteenth century. Late in 1848, the Royal Cyclorama and Music Hall in Regent's Park, London, mounted an exhibit of a legendary natural disaster, the great Lisbon earthquake of 1755. The quake had combined with fire and flood to obliterate most of the city in a day; so cataclysmic was the event that it has been credited with introducing European thought to the concept of nature as an impersonal, amoral force. To illustrate the innocent calm of the city before the quake, a mechanical organ played a selection from the *Pastoral*.

The date of the exhibition is suggestive. In the context of the revolutions that swept across Europe during that year, it would be hard not to discern a political earthquake hovering behind the imagery of a natural one. In that case the urban pastoral that began the exhibition would evoke the lost innocence of prerevolutionary Europe—something that the English, perhaps, needed to feel they could hold on to, even if the Continent couldn't.

Now to the movies. *Soylent Green*, an eco-catastrophe film of 1973, turns the narrative of the *Pastoral* Symphony inside out. It's all louring thunderstorm with a short musical sunbreak near the close. The film is set in a nasty urban dystopia fifty years in the future, a world where nature is extinct and food is distributed in pellets by the omnipresent Soylent Corporation. Citizens can get a glimpse of pastoral nature, though, and a good meal, if they're willing to be euthanized afterwards. Their chief pleasure is a movie full of gorgeous meadows and other pastoral imagery and the first movement of the *Pastoral* Symphony on the soundtrack.

One of the two leads, the sagelike figure Sol (read Solomon) Roth (Edward G. Robinson), is old enough to remember the world as it was. Eventually, the memory drives him to volunteer for the euthanasia program. The movie audience thus gets to watch him watch the movie-within-a-movie as it spins out the pastoral fantasy with Beethoven's help. Sol's death makes the illusion permanent. Unlike the real-world moviegoer, he does not have to reassume the critical or ironic distance he has cast off. The burden of that distance passes to the viewer over his shoulder, who, thanks to the context principle, can never wholly escape it.

On to television. In 1992, the animated Fox series *The Simpsons* broadcast an episode touchingly entitled "Itchy and Scratchy and Marge." Itchy and Scratchy are the postmodern Tom and Jerry: a cartoon cat and mouse pursuing mutually assured destruction on an absurdly violent TV show. After observing the show's appeal to her kids, especially the redoubtable Bart, Marge Simpson decides to do something about it and forms a watchdog group. Her efforts succeed: Itchy and Scratchy are canceled. The children of Springfield—having nothing else to do—take to the streets to play, just as kids used to do in the good old days. As we watch their innocent gambols, we hear the first fifty-three measures of the *Pastoral* Symphony.

The scene is played straight, a fragment of *Fantasia* in modern dress. It even suggests a pointed effort to improve on the Disney version, which hovers a little ominously behind it. The music helps defer too quick a return to the satire signaled by the context. Even Bart Simpson hesitates to take on Beethoven. But it still comes as no surprise that the idyll is short-lived. Marge learns that her group's next target is the exhibition of an indecent statue: Michelangelo's David. She withdraws her support, and the Itchy and Scratchy show is soon renewed—just like that other, equally irreverent display of take-no-prisoners satire, *The Simpsons*.

Both *Soylent Green* and the *Simpsons* episode observe the principle of the silent background in a double sense: they conform to it, but they also scrutinize it, and with more than a little skepticism. We can't simply lose ourselves in Sol Roth's pleasure when we must watch him watch and overhear him hear; if we know *Fantasia*, we can't see the gamboling children of Springfield without seeing through them to Disney's centaurettes. This edge of discomfort is typical. Pastoral nostalgia often includes a potentially disruptive element of self-reflectiveness. This is perhaps a surprising turn, given the intent of pastoral fantasy to put skepticism and critical detachment to rest. But the point is to surmount skepticism, not ignore it.

From classical times to the present, this reflectiveness has centered on the intrusion into the pastoral world of something— anything: a force, a figure, a mentality—that ought to have been kept outside. Pastoral regularly incorporates the principle of violence that threatens to destroy it. It defines itself by a frailty that is paradoxically a source of strength. Vergil's *Eclogues*, ten poems published in 39 B.C. that furnished the West with much of its pastoral imagery, begin on a note of resentment. Roman politics disrupts the Arcadian countryside and throws the once carefree shepherds off their land. Arcadia comes into view at the point of loss. It lives mainly in memory or in the possession of others; its enjoyment must be either imaginary or vicarious. Nicholas Poussin's famous painting of 1640, *The Arcadian Shepherds* (figure 1), shows a quartet of pastoral figures puzzling over a tombstone bearing a legend from the Fifth Eclogue, "Et in Arcadia

Figure 1. Nicholas Poussin (1594–1665), *The Arcadian Shepherds (Et in Arcadia Ego).* Louvre, Paris, France. Photo credit: Reunion des Musées Nationaux/Art Resource, New York.

ego": "I'm in Arcadia too." The pastoral fantasy comes with a blot on the landscape, something indelible, like this memento mori. In the picture the blot is magnified, a hard central mass of brown stone indifferent to the suppleness with which Poussin renders both the shepherds' flesh and the surrounding country-side. And the blot is necessary. As Beethoven understood clearly, there can be no *Pastoral* Symphony without a thunderstorm.

The animators of *Fantasia* understood this too and tailored the *Pastoral* Symphony episode to cover the full narrative trajec-tory of the work's five movements. The episode forms a micro-cosm that models the whole movie, which repeatedly erupts in orgies of destructiveness: dinosaurs battling it out to Stravinsky's

Rite of Spring, an army of golemlike brooms unwittingly brought to life by Mickey Mouse as the Sorcerer's Apprentice to the music of Paul Dukas, and the culminating witches' sabbath joined with Musorgsky's *A Night on Bald Mountain*. We can only guess at how closely these violent episodes seemed to mirror the silent background, the desperate situation of Europe in 1940. Many Americans were in an isolationist mood and felt immune from the effects of what they perceived as someone else's war. But the people doing the fighting were also the people who made the music. The resonance is hard to ignore. At a minimum, the animation Americanizes the music and thus, in fantasy, cleanses it of the taint of European politics by bathing it in new-world innocence. At a maximum, the film's underlying rhythm models the idea of a Pax Americana capable of emerging from the ashes of Europe as tranquil music emerges from musical terror.

But emerges, in fantasy, without sacrifice. The trick of pastoral fantasy is to dispel violence rather than defeat it. Heroism is needless, even useless. All you have to do is wait. Memory is power; the shepherds will not cluster at that tombstone forever; the night will pass. *Fantasia* makes the point by concluding with a transition from *A Night on Bald Mountain* to Schubert's "Ave Maria"; as dawn breaks, evil dissipates under the daily triumph of light. And this brings us back to Beethoven's two symphonies of 1808.

The *Pastoral* Symphony in one sense represents a retreat from the militancy of the Fifth. It focuses the hope of the community not on a dynamic forward rush to victory but on a leisurely backward flow to the timeless peaceful countryside. Where the Fifth Symphony fantasizes taking control over history, the *Pastoral* fantasizes stepping beyond its borders. It's as easy as taking a walk beyond the city walls. The violence that follows regardless, that of the storm, may threaten the person it catches outdoors, but it can't threaten nature itself. The pastoral mode is safe.

The finale announces this by starting with real country music. It signals the end of the storm with a luminous *ranz des vaches*, a Swiss mountain air typically played on the alphorn, a wooden instrument audible across great distances. For Beethoven's generation, the sound of such a melody gave assurance that an age-old, elemental humanity could still be found, in harmony with nature, at the heart of modern Europe. The setting was usually the Alps, which carried a powerful mystique linking natural harmony with political liberty. When Rossini wrote the overture to his opera *William Tell* twenty years later—music well known to several generations of Americans from Warner Brothers cartoons and the *Lone Ranger* radio and TV series—he used exactly the same musical imagery. The sound of pastoral piping in the aftermath of orchestral violence has had remarkable staying power. The impression of hearing a lyrical call cross the distance is deeply reassuring, not only that all is well in the end, but that the ideal past lies somewhere in the geographical present, just over there. The distance comes right up close.

But so does the storm, which is meant to make us forget for a while that its danger is under control. The storm movement of the *Pastoral* Symphony is an extra. All the others correspond to standard slots in the four-movement symphonic format; this one does not. It actually is what it represents: a sublime intrusion. But it is linked to the music it disrupts by melodic transitions and mutations at both ends: it is, so to speak, an organic intrusion.

Here the power of detail comes vividly into play. Like the Fifth, the *Pastoral* discovers crisis in the passage between the major and minor modes of the same key, a primordial musical reality that anyone can hear. The key in this case is F, which in major is traditional for pastoral. The scherzo and its trio seem to be rolling along irrepressibly in an expanded cycle (scherzo-trio-scherzo-trio-scherzo) when distortions start to intrude. The second restatement of the scherzo takes a sour turn, barely recovers itself, and then plunges on toward a close. But instead of reaching its appointed final cadence in F major, the music collapses in a heap. The loud noise of celebration drops to virtual silence. Instead of the cadence a dissonant tremolo gurgles in the low cellos and basses. This ominous muttering breaks out in an otherwise silent space, as if everyone and everything had suddenly stopped dead. The music follows the course set by successive repetitions of this twanging. Meanwhile the strings begin to agitate and a little three-note figure suggests the first splotches of rain.

At this point we clearly know what the weather is. What we don't know is what the key is, and we won't know until the storm actually breaks some time later with a big fortissimo for full orchestra, including the debut boom of those previously silent kettledrums. The buildup is tense, inexorable. The tremolo rises incrementally, step by slow step, until the storm erupts on the keynote: D^b-D-E^b-E . . . F; the basses split off and grumble for the last two measures, ratcheting up the tension before the key and the thunder arrive together. The key we know—but it has turned to minor. Of course it has: this is a storm; it increases gloom. But the key also contains the principle of its own undoing, which will take the gloom with it. The F-minor outburst violently revokes the cadence deferred at the end of the scherzo, but it also substitutes for that cadence, continuing the very harmonic process it disrupts. The storm that is so disruptive is actually very lawful.

And the law it serves turns out to be a higher one, certainly natural, perhaps divine. As the storm abates, the anxious expectancy of its beginning turns to serene expectation. The F-major cadence we have been waiting for is just over the horizon. The preparation for it begins with the first appearance of the *ranz des vaches* on solo clarinet against a drone bass—a persistent open fifth, the traditional sound of pastoral harmony—on the violas. The transition becomes richer, more generative, as a horn repeats the call over blended string harmonies. The music finally crosses the threshold to the finale when the violins take over from the horn. The sonority is now collective, not individual; it has taken on warmth and body. The violins repeat the *ranz des vaches* and expand it into a full-blown melody, the song of thanks that is the main theme of the finale. They start with a tentative form of the long-awaited cadence and round to a sure one, so that we hear F major waxing as we have heard gloom wane. The moment restores the interrupted harmony of natural and social energies and enriches it with reflective awareness. The deferred cadence emerges just as the voice of the community takes up and transfigures the opening pastoral calls. The movement unfolds as the answer to those calls, which echo from within it every time the main theme is heard.

So everything connects. The festivity of the country folk musically evolves into the storm that shatters it, and the storm musically evolves into both the calm that follows it and the communal celebration of its passing. Pastoral crisis arises in transition and departs with transition. The storm, as I said before, is an organic intrusion. But why? Why not something with rough edges, a real disruption? Why not go for broke?

The answer lies in the wider displacement of political and historical crisis into the sphere of pastoral. The transitions establish

that the storm, disruptive though it is, is an integrated phenomenon. This is no Lisbon earthquake. It is part of the natural
cycle, and therefore not a true intrusion but the dark interim of
a passage that always leads back to light. The storm is in that
sense already over before it begins. It's the very model of the
force we learn not to fear: don't be afraid, we tell the children,
it's just thunder and lightning. We like a storm, says Kant in his
discussion of the sublime, when we're safe from it.

This cyclical integration paradoxically allows the storm
movement to be as realistic, as frightening, as furious, as the
music can make it. And furious it is: when Beethoven pulls out
the stops at the climax and introduces a pair of trombones,
exactly reversing their role in the Fifth Symphony, the noise is
still ear-splitting, and must have been much more so in its own
time. That's how Berlioz heard it, suggesting that this music
sounded very realistic indeed before being played and imitated
once too often. Rossini, Berlioz thought, did less well. His storm
music in *William Tell* is frightening, but it is more artifice than
art. We always sense its distance from what it depicts.

That's precisely what the art of Beethoven's transitions
enables us to forget. The realistic illusion of his storm claims the
authority of nature for an outcome ordained by convention, or
myth, or narrative tradition. These purely artistic sources can't
be denied, but they lack the compelling force of necessity. The
symphony will settle for nothing less. What its storm music says
is not simply that the storm can be weathered but that its weath-
ering is foreordained, inevitable. The very entry into crisis
means passage through crisis—say, political and historical crisis,
which have not been alluded to and might undermine the fantasy
if they were. We give ourselves over to the fantasy the moment

the storm sounds natural to us, all the while knowing perfectly
well that naturalness, too, is a convention.

The Fifth Symphony has no exact parallel to this, which is
one reason why the Sixth had to supplement it. The Fifth, too,
says that triumph, military, political, or what you will, is
inevitable and natural: that's why the transition from dark uncer-
tainty at the end of the third movement to brilliant clarity at the
start of the fourth is painstakingly slow and rigorously logical.
The finale shoots forth like a sunburst. But when the finale falls
back into conflict, then repeats the earlier transition in attenu-
ated form, its triumphant reemergence is necessarily compromised. The transition has done a great deal, but it cannot do
everything. The finale has to depend on a wildly extravagant
coda to carry the day. By common consent, the power of the
symphony's closing pages is overwhelming. We believe; we want
to believe. But there is a hole at the heart of this belief that the
symphony, no matter how often repeated, can never fill. The triumph of the closing pages is less an attainment than an imperative, and one that we cannot necessarily obey—in part because
we may lack the confidence and in part because of the peculiar
kind of imperative this is, the hardest kind of all to heed: *Enjoy
yourself! Feel pleasure! Keep your chin up!*

So a walk into the countryside becomes inevitable: it's a rescue mission. The order offered by pastoral, and the *Pastoral*, is
the only plausible counterweight to the buccaneering of the
Fifth Symphony. What makes it so is the familiar artifice of it all:
the fact that this pastoral order is understood as the stuff of a
durable cultural fiction, a collective fantasy. The resulting combination of unreality and inevitability gives the narrative of the
Pastoral a potency that no amount of heroic assertion can attain.

The point of saying so is not to prefer one symphony to another but to hear their resonance as a pair. What should we conclude from them about the kind of order we need, at a time of crisis, to support a reassuring fantasy? This would be an order that renders fantasy itself constructive rather than escapist. Fantasy in this guise is an imaginary scenario that teaches us how to dispose desire in the world and therefore how to think about the world. Such fantasy is not a denial of reality but a map of it.

In his essay. "Art for Art's Sake," written in 1949 with the memory of the Second World War still raw, E. M. Forster claims that the order required is the order of art itself. This is an order created in the place where politics, science, and religion have failed to create one. It is the order of art as a social and epistemic reality. But Beethoven, in my reconstruction of his voice of 1808, says something different. The order required is illusory rather than real. This is the order of an art that openly claims as fiction the idea that its order is the order of nature, and of nature in the most traditional sense, where all comes right in the end, including death and the sublime. This order has nothing overtly to do with the immediate causes of crisis, which is why it can represent a phantasmal remedy for them. And because this nature makes no attempt to hide its cultural supports—the mechanical organ for the Lisbon earthquake, the filmic apparatus in *Soylent Green*—it can't be debunked by revealing the machinery. It distracts us into our reassurance.

A question, then, a painfully obvious question: is our own post–September 11 form of this order that of a certain urban fantasy, an urban pastoral? Take, for example, the movie hit *Spider-Man,* conceived before the terrorist attacks but released in their wake. Based on a comic-book character, the film's superhero is really a classic loser, not just in disguise like Superman as Clark Kent. He's even told as much at one point: "You do too much. You're not Superman, you know." The real Spider-Man is a negative everyman. He's an embodiment of personal insecurity and inadequacy who happens to get bitten by a spider—another object of everyday fear, just like thunderstorms. But the spider has been genetically altered, and its bite turns out to be an enhancement that gives the unlikely hero the freedom of the city. Transformed into Spider-Man, ordinary Peter Parker can soar safely through the threatened sky of the threatened urban space, the skyline of Manhattan itself, and restore its beauty and romance, along with a purely manageable menace. Like Rodgers and Hart, Spider-Man knows a new way to say "I'll Take Manhattan." The results have a genuine bearing on a certain strain of musical pastoral even in the absence of audience overlap.

Chapter 1 alluded to an unscheduled performance of Brahms's *German Requiem* that Kurt Masur and the New York Philharmonic gave shortly after September 11. By all reports the music was powerfully affecting. One reason, I'm sure, is that its musical imagery combines sobriety with lyricism throughout, suggesting that tragedy can be confronted truthfully without losing the possibility of consolation. But the historical occasion of this performance urges us to seek out something more. The terms of these musical images are both biblical and pastoral ("And all flesh is as the grass"); the language is vernacular (German, not Latin); and the texture is primarily choral, with the rare solo appearances fully integrated with the chorus. These elements add up to an affirmation that the community of Western values is still intact and can still make sense of what had just so unthinkably happened. The music acknowledges a tragedy in terms deliberately drawn from the world that the tragedy has changed, perhaps forever. It thereby constitutes an affirmation that the culture and tradition under threat have the wherewithal to survive, to instruct, and to console.

The New York Philharmonic also commissioned a new work to commemorate the event. Vernacular speech also plays a key role in John Adams's *On the Transmigration of Souls*, which involves both a recitation of the names of the dead and readings, some spoken, some sung, from the "missing" posters that went up around the city in the days and weeks following the attack. The work is a musical portrait of the city in the grip of that long moment, and it incorporates real-world sounds within its musical fabric.

The musical imitation of external soundscapes is a familiar device with an intriguing category difference: evocations of the countryside tend to refer to specific sonorities (birdsong, a horse's gallop, the babbling of a brook), while evocations of the city involve nonspecific rhythm and energy, a general hustle and bustle. Gershwin's use of taxi horns in *An American in Paris* is an exception. The horns are the urban equivalent of cowbells—and so not as far removed from Beethoven's *ranz des vaches*, that is, cow call, as one might think. They anchor the work to the reality of what it depicts; they bring the modern urban world directly into the music.

Adams does the same thing more emphatically, and in a climate of elegy (also a pastoral genre) far removed from the movable feast of Paris in the 1920s. *Transmigration* finds a music in the actual soundscape of New York and first absorbs it, then transforms it, into symphonic sound. Voices, too, in retrospect suggesting "the still, sad music of humanity," transmigrate from ambient sound to choral enunciation; they become the music they contain. The recurrent intonation of the names of the dead, now spoken, now sung, offers the listener both the control of ritual and the release of catharsis. The process enacts a continuous transmigration of souls and sounds, of souls into sounds, and at the same time assimilates the musical work of transmigration to a traditional tragic form, indeed the oldest of tragic forms, the climactic, collective lament, a quasi-sacred utterance even in a purely secular context. The music thus affirms the continuing value of Western ways of life and spirit, both mundane and transcendental, in much the same way as the Brahms Requiem was able to do in the face of the same calamity.

The obvious incongruity between these painful yet consoling compositions and pop-cultural phenomena like *Spider-Man* should not prevent us from recognizing that all three works—the Brahms, in context, included—draw deeply on the contemporary logic of pastoral fantasy. Nor are they alone. The need to mobilize that fantasy after 9/11 was widespread.

Perhaps no medium could do so better than series television, which forms part of the texture of everyday life over long stretches of time. So consider the announcement in spring 2002 of a sizable group of retro TV programs for the fall season. The network executives were at pains to deny that the development of these series had anything to do with September 11, though one did admit that they "resonate" with it. The resonance has less to do with the actual shows than with their packaging. What counts above all is the fantasy promised, whether or not the fantasy is actually delivered. Or rather the packaging is the delivery; it tells the viewer how to process as fantasy what are likely to be the rigidly conventional narratives typical of network TV.

The most anticipated of these programs, NBC's family drama *American Dreams*, begins its narrative in 1963. The program is set in Philadelphia, the home of the era's daily rock 'n' roll variety show *American Bandstand*, which featured local teenagers dancing to the latest hits. Dancing on *Bandstand* is presented here through a veil of nostalgia as one of the American dreams that make up the grand, all-encompassing American Dream. One of the slogans used by the network to plug the new program spells out the pastoral premise of its title: "Remember the Innocence. Remember the Music."

There is more to this slogan than its unabashed sentimentality. Among the things I can remember from those days are the space race, Cold War nuclear anxiety, the Cuban Missile Crisis, the ominous beginnings of the Vietnam War, race riots, and the Kennedy assassination. In its guise as soap opera rather than musical memory tour, the show is about all these things, as the first episode announces by ending with the most iconic of them, the assassination. What makes it possible for this terrible moment in the past to be constructed retroactively as a time of innocence is precisely its safe distance from a present-day trauma that was, we're asked to believe, inconceivable from within the earlier frame of reference. The inconceivability is the innocence. Not even the Kennedy assassination could prepare us for September 11; softened by distance in time, the earlier trauma actually preserves the innocence it seems to have shattered when it really happened.

Another promotional spot for the show used a different slogan, heard as a voiceover: "Follow a family through the decade that changed us all." But the imagery contradicts the message of change: it highlights the *Bandstand* topic and even promises clips from the original show in living black-and-white. (The program complies; it regularly intercuts original footage with reconstructions of singing and dancing on *Bandstand*, complete with impersonations of yesterday's rock stars by current idols.) The imagery revives the time of innocence with the help of music: music, which seems to live but does not change. *Soylent Green* does exactly the same thing, right down to the familiar image of "dancing" meadows. The only difference is that it identifies the lost past with the present of the viewing audience. Sol Roth is the young viewer grown old, and more broadly the image of a world grown old and exhausted. Unlike Sol, though, prospective viewers of *American Dreams* do not have to pay a heavy price to revisit the time of innocence, the time of music. Whenever they want to, all they have to do is dream.

Another example of the same pattern—to revert to high art, but with a twist—is Charles Ives's *A Symphony: Holidays*, mostly composed between 1909 and 1913. This work is a compilation of four independent tone poems to form a seasonal cycle, à la Vivaldi, depicting four patriotic holidays as they were celebrated in nineteenth-century New England after the Civil War. Ives makes the typical identification of pastoral place with a lost time. The musical holidays are full of nostalgia for the 1880s of his boyhood.

This era was just a little less removed from Ives at the time of composition than the Kennedy era is from us today, well within living memory but utterly out of reach. What had intervened was not a single event but a seismic shift in culture. Ives let himself forget, or perhaps did not want to remember, that this shift had already started by the 1880s, but what affected him most was its scale two decades later. Fueled by industrial development and immigration, a heterogeneous urban world had encroached on a homogeneous rural one and replaced it as culturally dominant. Northern pastoral—Walt Whitman's "far-stretching beauteous landscape, / The roads and lanes, the high-piled farm-wagons, and the fruits and barns"—remained symbolically identified with the life of the nation and its essential innocence, but the symbolic bonds were already fraying badly. The sources of national identity were receding from everyday life; fading traditions could no longer guarantee the feeling of community. Ives's musical holidays try to arrest, or even reverse, these losses by reinventing the outdated world as cultural memory. At least the earlier and later worlds had the holidays in common. By reenacting in music the holidays as they once were, Ives could refresh their communal roots even in a deracinated present.

Basic to this effort is the recollection of the music heard at the old festivities. Ives needed that music the way Beethoven needed the *ranz des vaches*. No less than *American Dreams*, he could take as a motto "Remember the Innocence. Remember the Music." But the memory itself is not innocent. It is carefully framed against the silent background of social upheaval and the unresolved legacy of the Civil War. (Ives makes sure the legacy hovers. The second holiday, and the most pensive, is Decoration Day, the day of remembrance for the Civil War dead that became Memorial Day.) The memory is framed, too, by brooding preludes and fading postludes that invest the long-ago music with remoteness, so that we understand it as something remembered, not just something heard.

And there is plenty to remember. Ives, whose music is famous for quotation, saturated the cycle of symphonic holidays with a medley of Americana: folk songs, hymns, patriotic marches, dances, Stephen Foster tunes, the music of the Civil War, and

parlor songs. The medley culminates at the end of the last holiday, "Thanksgiving and/or Forefathers' Day," when a full chorus joins in with a traditional hymn linking the Pilgrims' voyage,
the origin of pastoral America, to divine providence: "God!
Beneath thy guiding hand / Our exiled fathers crossed the sea."
Music in this role is an anachronism that doesn't date.

The *Pastoral* Symphony lays claim to the same anachronism.
Even though the music claims to be more about a shift in space
than one in time, its pastoral theme does implicitly hark back to
an earlier generation. It conjures up an era that has not yet
received the skeptical message of the Enlightenment, with the
attendant burdens of heightened individuality and political insta-
bility. The community invoked by the symphony enjoys an
unbroken continuity of tradition. Its members unite in the aftermath of trauma by subsuming their individual identities in a
common hymn of thanksgiving, the melodic heart of which is a
communal expression rooted in the cyclical rhythms of nature.
Ives's Thanksgiving chorus seeks much the same condition.
Seeks, invokes—nothing more: the world in which that condition is possible no longer exists for either composer, if it ever
existed at all. Beethoven and Ives can imagine it only because
they can never have been part of it. Yet perhaps there are times
when imagining it is enough.

Imagining it, that is, in music. As Sol Roth or the builders of the
London Cyclorama could tell you, as Ives declares and Beethoven
intimates, the pastoral scene is always a scene remembered—
musically. The music involved is both an object of memory and a
means of remembering. This is one reason why the pastoral tradition so often invokes the sounds of the shepherd's song and the

shepherd's pipe and why it represents pastoral poetry as above all musical. From the eighteenth century on, and increasingly with the development of modernity, real music takes the place of these age-old musical metaphors. Pastoral thrives when music reflects without irony on its own past. This past is a strange one, a past that is always present but without its world, like a voice without a body. Regardless of the style involved, music enters the pastoral mode when it recalls a lost sound to life—but also recalls the loss.

In this process, the *Pastoral* Symphony served as both a model and a soundtrack. And in this context, the rock 'n' roll of *American Bandstand*—the golden oldies heard on each episode of *American Dreams*—shares a purpose with the older Americana of Ives's medley. There are differences, of course; the oldies come back whole cloth, while the medley is fragmented and distorted by time and cultural distance, but musical nostalgia is an object of faith for both. In a sense the *Bandstand* music is even more nostalgic, differing, as it does, from today's rock, alternative, and hip-hop by its purely acoustic production, unmediated by rhythm tracks, synthesizers, playback loops, and sampling. On the original show, its own technological apparatus (and its often lip-synched performance) lay hidden, Oz-like, behind the fluid shimmer of dancing bodies. We're supposed to hear this as real human music, from the hand, from the throat, from the heart. Ives would have hated it, but he would have understood.

Much the same is true for the *Pastoral* Symphony, with its drone basses, the idealized peasant dance of its scherzo, and the *ranz des vaches* of its finale. This is music that envelops the present with the pastoral promise of the past. It does so with such power of illusion that for a moment we cease to mourn that the promises have not been kept, could not possibly have been kept, and were perhaps never even made. The premier art in modern times of crisis is music—the music of lost time.

Which, though, leaves us with a nagging question. In what sense would an object of high, if faded, cultural esteem like the *Pastoral* Symphony, or the similar objects that ride its coattails, like Ives's *A Symphony: Holidays*, be better than a real mass cultural product like *American Dreams?* Should we want or expect them to be? Does the question even make sense? Why does classical music still matter?

One answer would be that high-cultural products do more with their self-reflectiveness than the popular culture products tend to do. They incorporate a thoughtful self-distancing from their own fantasies, which are nonetheless offered without more irony than they can bear. This distancing puts the fantasy-engine of these works at a certain remove. We can partake of the fantasy, all right, but we are also offered the opportunity to think about what it means and even to be critical of it, and of ourselves. The popular works are less comfortable with ambivalence. They tend either to harden distance into irony or to contrive its disappearance. "Itchy and Scratchy and Marge" does the first and *Fantasia* does the second.

I think there's some truth to this view, though I would not want to devalue popular culture because of it. There is no point in tilting at that old windmill. But the distinction, allowing for overlaps and exceptions, does point to a significant difference in function.

The type of reflective distance typical of the high-cultural products enables them to enter into the formation of cultural memory on a higher plane than that of mere nostalgia. This distance allows music like the *Pastoral* Symphony to function as a continuing expressive and conceptual resource, not just as a handy allusion to the outdated but fondly recollected past. The *Pastoral* is in itself never what it is in the scenes from *Soylent Green* and *The Simpsons*. It is never just a simple image of a lost paradise, though it contains such an image, or several. Rather it is a dramatization of how such images are derived, preserved, and utilized. It is a model of how images from the past may be applied to the present in ways that indirectly but potently address the very issues in the present that make the past seem lost or naive or irrelevant.

The opening of the finale acts out this very process as the shepherd's song passes from the clarinet and horn to the strings. The solo winds suggest the sound of distant piping over the fields; the full-bodied string choir takes that sound into the unmistakable, reflective voice of the classical orchestra. What gives a special vitality to works like the *Pastoral* and the other Beethoven pieces of 1808 is that they can be said to be works of reflective understanding without for a moment ceasing to be works of art. Rather than say what cultural memory is or should be, they show what it may be. In the process, they pass the opportunity and responsibility of working out the possibilities to those of us who listen.

E. M. Forster offers some further perspective on this process. The title of his essay, "Art for Art's Sake," evokes Oscar Wilde and 1890s aestheticism. But Forster's real affinity is with Beethoven's era, and especially with the idealist aesthetics of Friedrich Schiller. Schiller maintains that artistic form leads us toward the realization of the ideal—a unity of knowledge, pleasure, and freedom—even if the concrete content of the artwork is indifferent or hostile to the ideal. Forster updates this notion with a simple substitution. The order of art does not lead to the ideal, he suggests; it is the ideal. This order is what distinguishes art from politics, science, and religion and gives it the social effectiveness that they conspicuously lack. That does not mean, however, that art promotes anything redemptive or grandiose, as it does in Schiller. Forster settles instead for small touches of human decency and genuine accomplishment. But his position is also a rebuke to the version of modernist aesthetics that is hostile to the idea of order as the essential element in art.

The style of high modernism is a reason to be skeptical of Forster's claims, and in the years since he made them other reasons have accumulated. It is difficult nowadays to regard form as innocent of the social and political qualities that influence content and that Forster condemns as failures. It is difficult, too, to regard aesthetic order as self-contained when we have learned to perceive it as saturated by a thousand codes, styles, influences, echoes, allusions, and cultural references. Yet despite this Forster is on to something, as anyone who has ever had the experience of losing oneself in a work of art, whether making it, witnessing it, or performing it, should be ready to acknowledge. Forster's position is hard to accept theoretically, but it is in constant everyday use pragmatically. The fiction or metaphor of aesthetic order is basic to the cultural practice of enjoying art. It is one of those false assumptions that, as Forster says elsewhere, "must be accepted as true if we are to go on eating and working and loving, and are to keep open a few breathing holes for the human spirit" in a world that is always threatening to stop them up.

Nothing requires that the acceptance of this necessity be blind. The last quotation dates from 1939, when war was plainly imminent; it comes from the essay "What I Believe," which also contains the famous-infamous line, "If I had to choose between betraying my country and betraying my friend, I hope I should have the guts to betray my country." Reflecting the gloom of the time, Forster concedes the rule of the mailed fist but finds reasons for hope in delaying its blows: "Force . . . is, alas! the ultimate reality on this earth, but it does not always get to the front. . . . I call [its absences] 'civilization' and find in such interludes the chief justification for the human experiment. I look the other way until fate strikes me." Like Schiller, Forster believes that the interludes of civilization are best filled up by art for art's sake in the special sense he has tried to give the phrase; unlike Schiller, he hopes for nothing more than that and is willing to find it enough. To that end, he borrows a parable drawn from the art he loves most, namely music.

The parable is the story of Wagner's *Ring* cycle, or more exactly a selective interpretation of it. Forster does not hesitate over this choice for an instant; for him, Wagner belongs to German civilization, not to Nazi barbarism. We may be tempted to dismiss this view as naive, even complicit; a part of Forster would agree with the judgment, though not with the dismissal. That, in fact, is the point. Fafner and Fasolt, the giants who build Valhalla, are as stupid as they are strong, and because they are "the catastrophe is delayed and the castle of Walhalla, insecure but glorious, fronts the storms." Fafner, who becomes a dragon after killing Fasolt, "coil[s] around his hoard, grumbles and grunts; we can hear him under Europe today; the leaves of the wood already tremble, and the Bird calls its warning uselessly. Fafner will destroy us." But Wotan defers that destruction again by creating the Valkyries, "symbols not only of courage but of intelligence." The Valkyries "represent the human snatching its opportunity while the going is good, and one of them even finds time to love. Brünnhilde's last song hymns the recurrence of love, and since it is the privilege of art to exaggerate, she goes even further, and proclaims the love which is eternally triumphant and feeds upon freedom, and lives."

Forster knows perfectly well that Valhalla is built on theft and shady dealing and that Brünnhilde's last song—in the immolation scene of *Götterdämmerung*—is sung in atonement for a murderous betrayal of love that she has herself committed. Writing in a milieu where a thorough knowledge of Wagner went without saying, he expects us to know these things, too. He is not saying that they do not matter. On the contrary, it is from their mattering very much indeed that the image of the building and the actuality of the song draw their power to touch and console. Their declarations of beauty and love are not objects of belief but fictions of belief. They exemplify the condition that Wallace Stevens identified as "the nicer knowledge of belief, / That what it believes in is not true." For Stevens as for Forster, and at about the same time, this necessary contradiction is best exemplified when "closely the ear attends the varying / Of [a] precarious music, the change of key / Not quite detected at the moment of change."

Forster's reflections bring us around to the *Pastoral* Symphony by the back door. The catastrophe looming audibly under Hitler's Europe is symbolized by the trembling of a pastoral world, the shaking of the leaves, the uselessness of a birdsong that could belong as much to the second movement of the *Pastoral* as to the second act of *Siegfried*. Fafner's grumbling and grunting bear the same message as the rumble and roar of Beethoven's storm. What we are supposed to believe is that the storm will surely break but that it need not break us. But we are supposed to believe it with the nicer knowledge of belief: to believe it as a fiction, to believe it in disbelief. To call on Stevens again, in a poem of 1940 named for the plaintive sound of the solo oboe (was he thinking of the famous oboe cadenza that momentarily stays the tumult in the first movement of Beethoven's Fifth?): "The Prologues are over. It is a question, now, / Of final belief. So, say that final belief / Must be in a fiction. It is time to choose."

The *Pastoral* Symphony is both an example and a manifesto of art for art's sake in Forster's sense because what it provides is a fantasy structure that not only can survive disbelief but virtually presupposes disbelief in order to operate. It thus escapes the condition that both limits the affirmative power of the Fifth Symphony and compels the rhetorical excess of that work's closing measures. Samuel Taylor Coleridge famously wrote of "the willing suspension of disbelief for the moment that constitutes poetic faith." The *Pastoral* manages to formulate a poetic faith without requiring the suspension of disbelief, willing or otherwise. And the music that can do that—can do it over a long span, in detail, while mobilizing the peculiar power of music to reanimate the feeling of past days or decades—is music we need. The music that can do that can confront traumatic change. Its power is modest, and temporary, but it is real. Such song will diminish gloom.

CHAPTER SEVEN

Persephone's Fiddle

The Value of Classical Music

The last chapter has shown how classical music addresses extra-ordinary events, but what about ordinary life? How does the music's visionary sweep fit into the everyday existence that pop-ular music knows so well how to touch and enrich in clear, unapologetic form? This is in a sense the ultimate form of the question of why classical music still matters. In that sense it is the question we have to end with.

If you work, as I do, in Manhattan, nothing could be more ordinary than taking the subway. Let's start there.

Anyone who frequents the New York City subway often sees people performing music for spare change—buskers, as the British call them, though the term's festive connotations rarely carry over onto the train platforms. Some of these performers are pretty bad; loud, off-key caterwauling is not hard to find. Some are pretty good, or better than that. Where I run into buskers the most, on the uptown platform of the Broadway line at Times Square, the players on Jamaican steel drums are often virtuosos with the mallets, and during a recent Christmas season a pair of trumpeters came daily to trade off a few familiar tunes, one taking the melody straight, the other improvising on it, with an exuberance undaunted by the rumble of wheels on steel. The trains left the trumpets unfazed.

Classical music is a rarity in these precincts, except for the occasional rendition of *Für Elise* on the steel drums or extracts from *The Nutcracker* at Christmastime. Here is a little anecdote about one of the exceptions.

It was early fall, the start of a new academic semester, and the performer on the platform—Times Square, my usual spot— looked like a music student trying to pick up some extra cash for books or scores. She was young, in her early twenties, blonde, attractive, and well dressed, which may help explain the unusual amount of attention she was getting from a crowd that in normal circumstances doesn't give a busker a second glance.

Or maybe it was the music. She was playing the opening Adagio of Bach's G-Minor Sonata for Unaccompanied Violin. She played through the sound of the trains that in passing drowned her out; she played with a remote look on her face, as if absorbed by the music or transported by it to a less exposed, less daunting place, or as if it could shield her from the humiliation of begging; she played with great skill but little expression, as if to do no more than was absolutely necessary to render the piece correctly, as if this were not the place for expression—not for her, not for Bach.

The result should have been a fiasco: a merely dutiful rendition of slow, difficult music, half of which could not even be heard. Instead it was close to magical. At least fifteen or twenty people gathered in a circle around the violinist and listened closely. They were paying attention. One or two decided to keep listening rather than board their train when it arrived. If you listened closely enough, you could even follow the thread of the music when a train rumbled by, though the sound of the violin at that point was more imaginary than real—a point I'll come back to. Most remarkably of all, perhaps, when the movement ended there was a moment of complete silence followed by a smattering of applause. That was new to me. No one listens that hard in the subway; no one applauds buskers. For at least some of the passersby, the routine of playing for pennies had turned into a concert.

How had it happened? It seemed unlikely that a phalanx of Bach lovers had somehow stumbled onto the platform. This was not, by all odds, music that most of its listeners knew or loved, yet it seemed to be exercising an Orpheus-like charm on them. Part of me wanted to think that's exactly what was happening. Part of me was skeptical, unwilling to indulge the wishful thinking of the other part. Both parts need to be heard from here.

Bach's solo violin compositions—he wrote six—ask a melodic instrument, the quintessential melodic instrument of Western music, to provide all the harmony its melody needs. Not only does it have to project a bass line while it sings without fumbling the melody, but it must also evoke a contrapuntal texture of up to four voices. This much is common musicological lore. The premise of these pieces is a formidable exercise of technique. But what does the exercise mean? What does it do? Why is it important?

One good answer is that it dramatizes a triumph of spirit over matter. The enterprise is in keeping with Bach's theology, but it obviously has a wider resonance. The music asks its instrument to transcend itself. The listener is invited to bear witness. Note here follows note in a continuous current, intense, energetic, disciplined, unremitting, a process as perceptible in the motions of the player's bow arm as it is in the sound the bow draws from the strings. The shape of the melody, the contrapuntal interplay, the movement of the bass, all emerge distinctly from the forceful current of sound but without becoming fully detached from it. The ear knows that what it hears is partly its own inference, an ideal form, at its most intense a kind of epiphany. But it also knows that the current is thickly, richly material, and that the pattern is revealed only through the expert manipulations of arm and finger, of string and bow, the body of the performer spiriting itself into the body of the instrument. If the manipulations fail, the result is unseemly, a squawk or screech with nothing to cover it. If the manipulations succeed, the result is music of naked Orphic power. Differences of technology aside, to play this music against the rumbling of subway trains is not at all inappropriate; it's insightful.

The part of me touched directly by this epiphanic triumph wants to say that the others on the platform were touched in the same way. It didn't matter whether they could recognize the composer or the music or whether they cared about "classical" music deeply, casually, or not at all. Genius will out; the music simply revealed itself with a splendor nothing could subdue. The unlikely conditions of the performance were more help than hindrance. Their heavy weight of mundane matter, their burdens of mass and money and movement, proved oddly forgettable when spirit unexpectedly blew in.

But the skeptical part of me doesn't like talk of forgetting. Its sometimes annoying vigilance includes having a good memory, and what it remembers here is that the experience I have been describing in quasi-metaphysical terms is also, and originally, a social experience. It matters (to work the word again) that the violinist was a pretty middle-class white girl. It matters that she was playing a violin. And it matters that the music would probably be recognized as "classical" even if it weren't recognized as Bach, and that this recognition would invite forms of behavior quite different from those invited by more familiar, more "popular" forms of ambient music. Even if I really did witness a small triumph of spirit in the hurly-burly of a busy day, in a busy place, the triumph had to have a practical means of realization. There had to be a social equivalent to the musical technique utilized and demanded by the sonata. What happened may have been magical, but it wasn't magic. So it's necessary to ask why this music, the values it embodies aside, got the reception it did between the local and the express tracks on a random Monday morning.

Three possible reasons come to mind, each of which seems to offer insights that go beyond this particular episode of busking and by so doing render it the more exemplary. The reasons involve, respectively, the psychological, social, and cultural dimensions of listening to the Bach sonata, both in the subway and elsewhere. It will come as no surprise that these categories constantly overlap. What I hope does come as a surprise is the turn taken by some of the traits familiarly associated with classical music and its advocacy.

The first reason is the need to pay attention. If the passersby were going to hear this music at all, they had to stop passing and listen. In fact they had to listen especially hard. They had to act as William Wordsworth imagined himself doing in 1805, turning aside from his path to hear a girl sing a haunting song as she reaped, a solitary figure, in a Highland field:

Alone she cuts and binds the grain,
And sings a melancholy strain.
O listen! For the vale profound
Is overflowing with the sound.

All classical music is designed to be heard attentively, but this piece of Bach's and its like demand attention where many others simply invite it. And even the invitation is a kind of demand: people know that classical music is *supposed* to be listened to in a certain way, with a certain ritualized respect, quietly, on one's best behavior. More "popular" types of music are more attuned to movement; they are something one moves to, not something one grows still for. People in the subway can literally take such music in stride. With music like this Bach, one can only stride away. Performed in an open public space, Bach's Adagio issued a call to social order within which its demand for higher-order attention nestled unobtrusively, hand in glove.

In Bach's day, this demand was partly pedagogical and partly spiritual. The music was written for performers, not for audiences; it isn't originally concert music. Striving to meet the challenges of technique, all learning and experience brought to bear, the violinist listens to confirm success or record failure. But in the process—all music, for Bach, being dedicated *ad maiorum gloriam Dei*, to the greater glory of God—the same violinist undergoes a spiritual discipline and through that discipline achieves a spiritual elevation. A principal model for this enterprise may have been the biblical figure of David the psalmist, who (as we saw in chapter 5) would later play a similar role in the imagination of Robert Schumann. According to the commentary printed in Bach's personal copy of the Bible, David ordered the worship service not through his own initiative but "through the

model that the Lord placed before him by his spirit." To which
Bach added in his own hand: "Besides other arrangements of the
worship service, music too was especially set in order by God's
spirit through David." Music is a divine gift, but it is also a divine
labor, a setting in order that can be accomplished only by the
musician's devoted service.

With all Bach's pieces for unaccompanied violin, intense
effort comes to fruition in self-surrender. Violinists today still
talk about the experience of playing the music in these terms; so
do cellists who perform Bach's solo suites for their instrument,
another set of six. When later centuries decreed that such pieces
would be concert music after all, audiences were called on to partake of this process vicariously. There are dangers in doing so, of
course, risks of credulity, secondhand edification, obsequious-
ness, mere attitudinizing. But there are also the possibilities of
emulation and insight—and something more.

The idea of music set in order by God's spirit through David
draws on one of the oldest notions about music, a literally classical—ancient Greek—conception here absorbed into the biblical
tradition. Harmonious sound had been treated as an image of
cosmic harmony ever since Pythagoras discovered the arithmeti-
cal principles underlying the octave. The notion was later Chris-
tianized by application to the Creation story; the logos, God's
creating Word, became identified with the fabled music of the
spheres, "that undisturbéd song of pure concent," as Milton
memorably called it. The harmony of the inner person then
became an echo of that song. David the psalmist provided a sublime model for this image, becoming a kind of biblical Apollo.

Bach gives this conception an important twist that much later
music would follow. Bach the contrapuntalist does not identify

cosmic harmony, be it inner or outer, with concord or consonance. On the contrary, his music is highly dissonant; and although the dissonances are resolved in the contrapuntal process, the music's order is at least as much about producing as resolving them. Its ethos is dissonance shaped into pattern and consummated therein, the very pattern that the ear strives to apprehend in the solo sonatas against the material density of the sounds. T. S. Eliot, invoking the sound of the violin, describes the result as a stillness made of motion: "Only by the form, the pattern, / Can words or music reach the stillness, as a Chinese jar still / Moves perpetually in its stillness." For Bach, though, this contemplative rapture is only a means, not an end, for the wayfaring spirit. The performer's, and later the listener's, absorption in the endeavor to achieve this stillness presses intently forward toward a state where contemplation itself becomes a mode of action. For one of Bach's contemporaries and a fellow Davidite, the English poet Christopher Smart, the aim is a condition in which the heart, "in all things where it was intent," becomes capable of "answering true to true." Smart's "A Song to David" of 1759–63 describes the result as a motion from stillness to stillness: "Where ask is have, where seek is find, / Where knock is open wide."

Later the mode of attentiveness associated with this exalted state would take on new meanings as it encountered historical circumstances closer to our own. With the rise of full-blown modernity in the later nineteenth century, the faculty of attention took on new prominence. It was conceptualized with a greater clarity, given a greater importance, and charged with a more vital function than ever before. Attention became the instrument by which the self met the social demands of modern life or was undone by them.

In a famous essay of 1903, "The Metropolis and Mental Life," the German sociologist Georg Simmel drew out the consequences of the widespread feeling that modern life in the cities of the West was fraught with too much perceptual stimulation, one result of which was a loss of both the power and the opportunity to concentrate one's attention. This was not a byproduct of modernity but its essence, the consequence of the drastic speeding up of work, transportation, and communication that would repeat itself a century later in digital form. Beset at "every crossing of the street" by the "tempo and multiplicity of economic, occupational, and social life," accosted by "the rapid telescoping of changing images, pronounced differences within what is grasped at a single glance, and the unexpectedness of violent stimuli," the citizen of the modern metropolis develops a hard defensive shell, a "blasé" attitude that serves as a shield against distraction or paralysis. Attention is withheld, husbanded; just enough goes out to the world to avoid being injured by it. The "metropolitan person" is thus removed to "a sphere of mental activity which is the least sensitive and which is the furthest removed from the depths of the personality."

It so happens that just at the time these ideas were crystallizing, a major Bach revival was crystallizing, too. And the grounds were much the same. Bach was celebrated as the creator of pure music at its purest, the model for all the rest: music that both demanded and richly rewarded the repose of attention in its musical devices, above all in its contrapuntal depths. This development was the culmination of a nearly century-long advocacy of a style of listening in which being wholly absorbed in the musical artwork was equal to being wholly enthralled by it. Music thus emerged as the location of attention that seemed to have vanished everywhere else. Listeners to a composition could compose themselves through their listening. In music they could find a replacement for the "slower, more habitual, more smoothly flowing rhythm of the sensory-mental phase of small town and rural existence" from which, for Simmel, the modern metropolis had alienated its inhabitants. And in this imaginary pastoral they could become reconnected to "the unconscious levels of the mind [that] develop most readily in the steady equilibrium of unbroken customs." Where music is found, the organic society has not quite been lost. The lost song of the solitary reaper can revive in the violin solo of the subway busker.

Simmel may represent a nostalgia for a life that never was, but the power of music to compose the self by orchestrating the listener's attention, and thus to give the old ideas of cosmic harmony and Davidite enrichment their distinctive modern form, is real enough. And there is no need to claim ideological innocence for it in order to value it. Nor does its value depend on a model of submissive or purely musical listening; on the contrary, more engaged, more imaginative, more informal styles of listening make it work all the better. Idealizing the powers of attentive listening and the music that sustains it is a historical occurrence, but the powers themselves are also historical discoveries. They can continue to work amid changing times; they can still matter as much as they ever did. They certainly seemed to be alive and well in the Times Square subway station when my classical busker charmed a crowd of hardened blasé passersby into attentive listeners. Her playing, and what she played, palpably dissolved a now-routine form of urban alienation and replaced it, for a few minutes, by something that Simmel and his generation were ill prepared to recognize, a cosmopolitan idyll.

A second perspective on this idyll opens up if we shift our focus from the psychological to the social effects of paying attention to Bach. Here we encounter the second possible reason for the music's surprising success in the subway. The busker's Bach lifted those who listened to it out of mundane life. By this I don't mean that the music provided an antidote to emptiness, alienation, or banality. It condescends to too many people, all the familiar strangers and strange familiars such as one meets on the train platform, to assume that their everyday lives are like that. Rather, what the music did in an exemplary way was to reorient its listeners from the unexceptional to the exceptional. In so doing it invited them to think freshly about the values of both.

Going beyond the mundane is part of the expressiveness of this particular solo sonata, but it is also representative of a more general function. The effect is consistent with Bach's Davidite aesthetic, but its import is not explicitly theological, merely harmonious with a worldview emphasizing the distractions of common self-interest and the need to surmount them in the service of more general values. The underlying conception is of the mundane as the scene of fallible life, swayed too much by both the vanity of worldly purposes and the vanity of the persons who pursue them. More modern conceptions may add elements of social and psychological alienation and, more recently still, the subjective fragmentation associated with digital and wireless technologies, but the guiding idea is of a sphere of life that needs to be periodically startled out of its self-preoccupation and into self-forgetfulness. Thus lost, the self can be found again in less selfish form through absorption in something other, in which others, too, can become absorbed.

The sonata offers a departure from mundanity in this sense to the performer first of all, who gains it through self-abnegating concentration on technique. The listener can take up the same offer by giving the music concentrated attention, which it rewards with an emotional complexity—stately yet impassioned, lofty yet intimate—that links eighteenth-century spiritual discipline and its rewards with modern interiority. As early as 1771, the Swiss philosopher Johann Georg Sulzer had generalized this link by endowing musical attention with spiritual power. Confronted by music that combines emotional richness with richness of technique, "the attention is totally held by the play of harmony, and the ear is induced into a state of complete self-forgetfulness, so that it concentrates only on the refined emotions that take possession of the soul." The focal point here is the emotions themselves, not the passing individual who feels or recognizes them, and the emotions are indistinguishable from the "play of harmony" that holds the attention when the listener is all ears.

So it was in the subway: this performance was received appreciatively because it induced self-forgetfulness, which in this place and time meant that it suspended the cares and rhythms of the morning's business. The suspension was literal fact; the music turned people aside from their comings and goings and momentarily took possession of them. It did so because the performance itself was out of the ordinary—not your usual busking—and because the music performed and the skill needed to perform it were extraordinary (the violinist could have chosen something less demanding both to play and to hear). The crowd in the station was thus offered a chance for the social performance of the inner life. They did so by the way they listened and the way they gathered to listen. Some, as noted, even chose to miss their trains as part of their own performance. They let the world go by.

Such performance suspends mundane activity but makes no pretense of leaving it behind. On the contrary: the conjunction of the extraordinary and the mundane offered the listening passersby the opportunity to validate the mundane by its very proximity to the extraordinary. It gave them the chance to experience the depth of the inner life—by which I mean to enact it, to produce it, to rehearse it in a public context—as the very thing that renders the mundane worth our allegiance and our service, however differently that inwardness may be defined for each separate listener. From this perspective, the music did not—does not—negate or escape the historical conditions of modern life, but enacts a relation of mutuality between the practical and idealistic dimensions of life under those conditions, which it acknowledges as inescapable.

This social performance, fully consolidated by the end of the nineteenth century, is the appointed work of classical music and of its own rituals, those of playing an instrument, concertgoing, private listening, and so on. And what works in the concert hall apparently works in the transit system. The busker's Bach did not so much cause the break in routine of the subway passengers as permit that break, which was signified, as such breaks normally are, by a ritual formation, here the listening circle, the silence, the applause. On this occasion, since the social force of the musical genre was clear, the passersby took their assurance from a music of which some, at least, perhaps most, would not normally avail themselves.

It is essential here that the musical performance was live and that the performer belonged to a valued social type. Ambient classical music in airports and train stations is just as much acoustic wallpaper as any other type, except perhaps as a call to

order: the musical image of high civilization imposes the responsibility of civility, and incidentally—given the temper of the
times—affirms Western values under threat and helps drive off
homeless people, who seem to be shamed by it. The reception of
the busker's Bach was in part a response to her person (she was
appealing, nonthreatening, easily idealized) and in part a response
to her skill (her years of training were reflected in every phrase,
every stroke of the bow). On this basis, the musician and the listeners entered into a spontaneous social contract in which the
ritual performance of each became the mirror image of the
other's inner life.

It is not a problem that these performances have an economic
basis, as the open violin case, calling to be fed by coins and bills,
makes eloquently clear. On the contrary: the exposure of that
basis in the subway performance is refreshingly honest. It clearly
indicates several of the social problems surrounding classical
music. How do we locate this music on the social map, especially
in relation to ourselves, and how do we free the music from the
social constraints that threaten to alienate it from the wider community? The social drama of this little anecdote is exemplary.
Youth and middle-class status are no guarantees of good fortune;
the spirit can provide sustenance only if the flesh receives it.
Singing for one's supper is no disgrace. Superstar musicians of
every persuasion do it every day; Johann Sebastian Bach did it his
whole adult life.

The ritual element introduces the third reason for the music's subway enchantment, this one the most important and problematic of
all. What enabled the busker's Bach to convene a social ritual and
at the same to issue a successful call for concentrated attention?

The answer is obvious enough: this music is heavyweight. It carries cultural authority. Under the right circumstances, it can even carry that authority to people who are otherwise indifferent to it.

Here again Bach's Davidite aesthetic is paradigmatic. The music poses, and exposes, the risks and rewards of hearkening to the voice of authority—a sense of exaltation on one hand and of servility on the other. As the Russian literary theorist Mikhail Bakhtin suggested, reverence toward a set form of exalted utterance, be it a political credo, a hymn, or any other "authoritative word," enhances the risk by absorbing the force of servility into the form of exaltation. To counteract this, the individual needs to reformulate the utterance with "interiorly persuasive speech," by means of which the utterance can be applied, transformed, subverted, or, for that matter, revalidated. In this respect, too, the subway performance is exemplary: it harnesses the force of the music as authoritative word, but it also shows how to limit that force and resist the excesses of that authority, to criticize and revise their mandates. It enables the attentive listener not only to answer true to true but also to pose the questions that must be answered truly. The music may be exalted, but that doesn't mean it can't be performed underground. It doesn't even mean the listener can't be irreverent. In this new venue, there is no room for solemnity or pomposity. Listening is optional; the music, like the performance, begs as much as it calls and will gratefully take what meaning it is given. Which is only what it always does, or should do, if we're honest about it. Classical music turns deadly when we venerate it. It comes to life when we hear it, whenever and wherever we do, as busking writ large.

The stakes in such listening can be high. A good example, none the less truthful for being fictitious, will carry us from the

Times Square subway to the White House—the television White House of the NBC drama series *The West Wing*. But we will not travel far from Bach and his music for unaccompanied strings. The music we know already.

In an episode entitled "Noel" (2000), the senior staffer Joshua Lyman (Bradley Whitford) is forced to consult a psychiatrist (Adam Arkin) to deal with the posttraumatic stress of having been shot nearly to death. During the day he has been moody and ill-tempered. The night before, in his apartment, he thrust his arm palm up through a window and severely gashed his hand, but he pretends to others—and to himself—that he accidentally cut himself when setting a glass tumbler down too hard. The "accident" occurs after his return home from a White House Christmas concert at which he was inexplicably traumatized by hearing Yo-Yo Ma perform the Prelude to Bach's Suite for Unaccompanied Cello in G Major. Eventually, he will discover that the music has merged in his mind with the sound of the sirens he heard in the wake of being shot; his breaking of the window is a semisuicidal gesture that reenacts the shooting but displaces the bloody wound from his torso to his hand. His escape from this deadlock, which is hard won, comes via a climactic movement toward psychological self-recognition, following the classical Freudian formula: he has to remember the trauma without reliving it. He has to retrace the path of pain from the shooting to the concert to the window and back again. And the turning point in this process, the recovery of the scene at the window, coincides precisely with the climax of the music, heard on the soundtrack and also, it is suggested, in Lyman's unconscious memory.

In the moments before his breakthrough, the unacknowledged association of the musical sound and the sirens—the ultimate trigger and the key to the mystery—is made explicit on the soundtrack amid flashbacks of the shooting intercut with the concert. But this only happens in passing, almost by the way, and is confirmed only after the impassioned and cathartic close. The final recognition does not take place during the music but only after it, upon reflection, a reflection that the first recognition, that of breaking the window, makes possible. Breaking the window thus changes retrospectively from an act of desperation and self-deception to the symbolic shattering of a barrier to self-possession and insight. And the barrier is transparent because one only has to look, or listen, through it to grasp the truth. The music has been telling the truth all along.

"Noel" understands that the Prelude has other meanings than this, and other than those we met with early in this book in connection with the films *Master and Commander* and *The Pianist*. There are subtle resonances to connect these meanings—the sense that this music belongs to a world free of violence, the sense that it is nonetheless, and therefore, as vulnerable as glass—but the music renews and transforms its meaning to meet each new circumstance that it encounters. "Noel" makes a point of this fluidity. What the music means for Yo-Yo Ma and the psychiatrist is far from what it means for Lyman—closer to the abounding delights of *Master and Commander*'s Galapagos than to the receding dream of *The Pianist*'s Warsaw. Ma embodies the spirit of the Davidite performer. As he plays the camera dwells on the serenity of his face and the graceful motions of a body in perfect control, in pointed contrast to Lyman's turmoil and his self-inflicted wound. The music, says the psychiatrist, is "a nice piece"; the reaction shots of the audience say it is even more, that it is beautiful, exalting, and far from the world's troubles. But that the music genuinely assumes the meanings it has for Lyman is equally clear, and that its authority is fully realized precisely by its ability to do so, by its unimpeded movement from one set of meanings to another, is equally clear.

There is a profound two-way communication here. What the music is saying about the drama is that there is a relentless force pressing Lyman to release his trauma, which he can do only if he stops resisting it. Thus the piece is played in its entirety throughout the six-minute scene, a real rarity for television, but with an interruption for an intense dialogue between Lyman and his therapist, under whose pressure he does in the end yield himself to the force of memory. At this point the music resumes and the flashback showing what really happened in his apartment begins. The music, suddenly ratcheting up its intensity, steadily mounts to its climax as the images show the breaking of the glass; the climax itself coincides with Lyman raising his bloodied hand to his face. The hand fills the screen. But this moment of remembered trauma is also the moment at which the music is released into its broad, suddenly serene conclusion, which we hear as the image changes to the sight of the bow on the soundboard and thereafter fades to white.

But the drama is saying something about the music, too, something shown in the shift in visual emphasis from the early moments of the concert scene, when the camera swirls around Yo-Yo Ma with emphasis on his tranquil, nearly expressionless face mixed with glimpses of rapt faces from his audience, to the scene's later moments, when the emphasis is on the never-ending, effortful movement of the bow on the strings. We no longer see Yo-Yo Ma, no longer see a celebrity performer; the movement of the bow arm is anonymous, impersonal. It could be a busker's arm, tuxedo-clad or not.

So there is, we're asked to see, something relentless about the music itself, something fiercely concentrated, unyielding, even a little obsessional, a knotted intensity that can release itself only by intensifying the performer's effort in a climactic and deeply consistent passage—a chromatic ascent—that is the transitional zone to release, repose, atonement. We grasp suddenly the significance of the fact that there is not a single rest in this music, that every second is filled, and that the note-motion never changes. These features are not unusual in Bach, but they are emphasized here by the cello's unbroken solo sonority and by the chromatic ascent itself, which spans more than the twelve tones of the octave over a steadily drumming bass note. The ascent starts on a dissonance, F natural, which must resolve to the F# of the key signature (technically the leading-tone, the note that ushers in the keynote), and thence to the keynote G. All of these things happen in the first few instants, but they happen in the middle of the bar, and in the bass. They carry no sense of finality. The ascent therefore has to continue, one chromatic notch at a time for as long as it takes, until the G falls on the downbeat, and in the treble, and so finds the point of *melodic* resolution from which the broad and flowing close can rightly flow, and flow aright. This music, like the violin sonata but in a darker vein, is seeking to redeem itself—from what who knows? guilt? mortality? original sin?—by embracing self-discipline without reserve. This is the discipline of performance, the morality of effort, almost an ethic of self-abnegation, for which the reward is a brief moment of pure ecstasy.

At its best, classical music is defined by the discovery, and the continual rediscovery, embodied by both Yo-Yo Ma's performance of the solo cello suite at the fictional White House and the unknown busker's performance of the solo violin sonata in a real subway station. This is the discovery that music attentively heard can become the performance of inner coherence. It can serve as the portal to an inner life understood as possessing a psychological and emotional richness that the ego enjoys and suffers but never fully masters—hence a life not wholly determined by mundane forces and responsibilities. (T. S. Eliot caught at this, too, in lines we've met before: "Music heard so deeply that you are the music / While the music lasts.") This life, or more properly this sense of life, is not a possession but an opportunity, not a presence but an activity. It offers an antidote to both the distractions of a complex world and the adaptations required to negotiate them. These things may no longer be as forbidding or alienating as they once seemed, but they are hardly enough to live on in a deeper sense. We still need something "slower" and more resonant. Music became "classical" in the nineteenth century—some of it retrospectively—to provide that something.

By the turn of the twentieth century, Bach (along with Beethoven) had become the model of what classical music in general is supposed to do. Bach as a web for attention is installed at the source of the "classical" tradition to which, in the strict sense dating from the later eighteenth century, he does not belong. This "pure" Bach is a retrospective construction based mainly on abstract pieces like the solo string sets and collections of preludes and fugues for keyboard. Such music seemed to reveal the transformative power of pure pattern independent of color or "effect" or rhetoric. To some extent this is just an illusion, a fiction that, at its worst, produces snobbery and affectation. As both the Times Square moment and *The West Wing* show, rhetoric and context are as much a part of this music as the notes. Venue matters; the performance and the performer matter; the meaning of the music is as dependent on its occasion as on its form. But as the same moments also show, the fiction can have spontaneous effects in which snobbery and affectation have no part. Insofar as the possibilities that such music harbors remain discoveries rather than temporary expedients, insofar as we can still feel them deeply—which is the litmus test—they still matter to us, to who we are and who we may be. That does not exempt them from political and social implications, or from criticism on those grounds. But such an exemption would be a declaration of irrelevance: things that matter are things we bother with.

And one reason why we bother is the music's power to bother with us. Despite its strict notation, the unchanging order of the notes, the music has the extraordinary capacity to fit itself to myriad circumstances, spanning the full distance—both material and social—between the sheltered precinct of a concert room and the labyrinth under the city's streets, between the undiscovered bounty of the natural world in the Galápagos Islands and the civilized world about to shatter like glass in Nazi-occupied Warsaw.

Despite the frigid connotations of its label, classical music of the kind exemplified by our Bach pieces is the very opposite of frozen in its presumed grandeur. Lend it an ear, and it will effortlessly shuck off the dead-marble aspect of its own status and come to as much life as you can handle. It will invite you to hear meanings it can have only if you do hear them, yet it will give you access to meanings you had no inkling of before you heard the music. It has nothing to do with the classic in the sense of a timeless monument that dictates a self-evident meaning and demands obeisance for it. It opens itself like a willing hand or smile, making itself available to you for self-discovery, reflection, and, yes, critique. And at times, as here, it will go further. It will offer you moments of revelation—however one wishes to take the term—that stay in the mind's ear with a resonance that, like the song of Wordsworth's solitary reaper, will not die out:

> I listened, motionless and still,
> And, as I mounted up the hill,
> The music in my heart I bore
> Long after it was heard no more.

REFERENCES

My intellectual indebtedness goes far deeper—even to the same people—than the few names cited below can suggest. Anyone's would. The past twenty years have been exceptionally rich in musical thinking and musical debate, which supply the context without which this book would not have been possible. My thanks go to all the participants, whether cited here or not, even to my critics.

CHAPTER ONE: CLASSICAL MUSIC AND ITS VALUES

002   Statistics. See Alan Kozinn, "This Is the Golden Age," *New York Times*, May 28, 2006, AR 1, 18.

011   Opera. Although this book sets it aside except for some passing mentions of Wagner, another does just the opposite: my *Opera and Modern Culture: Wagner and Strauss* (Berkeley: University of California Press, 2004).

013   Julian Johnson. *Who Needs Classical Music* (New York: Oxford University Press, 2002).

015 Structural listening. See "Toward a Deconstruction of Structural Listening: A Critique of Schoenberg, Adorno, and Stravinsky," in Rose Rosengard Subotnik, *Deconstructive Variations: Music and Reason in Western Society* (Minneapolis: University of Minnesota Press, 1996), 148–76.

016 In New Orleans. Stephen Kinzer, "As Tourism Halts in New Orleans, Musicians Play On," *New York Times*, September 25, 2001, E2.

020 "Simply myself." Jean-Jacques Rousseau, *The Confessions* (1764–70), trans. J. M. Cohen (London: Penguin Books, 1953), 17; translation slightly modified.

020– Categorical imperative. Immanuel Kant, *Groundwork of*
021 *the Metaphysics of Morals* (1785), trans. H. J. Paton (London: Hutchinson, 1948), 96.

029 Ludwig Wittgenstein. *Culture and Value*, ed. G. H. von Wright with Heikki Neiman, trans. Peter Winch (Chicago: University of Chicago Press, 1980), 51; see also 38, 83, and, perhaps most memorably, "A theme has no less a facial expression than a face" (52; my translation).

031 Carl Einstein. "Methodological Aphorisms," *October* 107 (2004): 147.

CHAPTER TWO: THE FATE OF MELODY

039 Poetry inspired by the late quartets of Beethoven. The first quotation from *Burnt Norton*, the second from *The Dry Salvages*, respectively the first and third of *Four Quartets*, in T. S. Eliot, *Collected Poems, 1909–1962* (New York: Harcourt, Brace, and World, 1963), 178, 199.

039 The same realization. Rainer Maria Rilke, *Sonnets to Orpheus*, trans. M. D. Herter Norton (New York: Norton, 1962), part 2, no. 13, p. 94; my translation.

052 Walter Benjamin. "Fate and Character" (1921), in *Reflections: Essays, Aphorisms, Autobiographical Writings*, ed. Peter Demetz (New York: Schocken Books, 1986), 308.

054 Matthew Arnold. "Memorial Verses," from *Poetry and Criticism of Matthew Arnold*, ed. A. Dwight Culler (Boston: Houghton Mifflin, 1961), 109.

057 Mary Douglas. *Purity and Danger: An Analysis of Concepts of Pollution and Taboo* (London: Routledge and Kegan Paul, 1966), 121.

060 Never happened—*yet*. Hugh McDonald recounts this anecdote in his "Schubert's Volcanic Temper," *Musical Times* 99 (1978): 949–52.

064 Otto Wagner. Quoted in Carl Schorske, *Fin-de-Siècle Vienna* (New York: Knopf, 1980), 74.

065 Nietzsche. From *The Case of Wagner* (1888), in *The Birth of Tragedy and The Case of Wagner*, trans. Walter Kaufmann (New York: Random House, 1967), 187.

CHAPTER THREE: SCORE AND PERFORMANCE

073 W. B. Yeats. "Among School Children," in *Collected Poems* (London: Macmillan, 1967), 245.

075 We can recognize a work of music. For a history and critique of this concept, see Lydia Goehr, *The Imaginary Museum of Musical Works: An Essay in the Philosophy of Music* (Oxford: Oxford University Press, 1992).

075 Shooting script. Nicholas Cook, "Music as Performance," in *The Cultural Study of Music*, ed. Martin Clayton, Trevor Herbert, and Richard Middleton (New York: Routledge, 2003), 204–14.

077 "... could scarcely believe their ears." Thomas Mann, *The Magic Mountain* (1924), trans. H. T. Lowe-Porter (New York: Knopf, 1967), 637; translation slightly modified.

077 Catalog copy for the . . . Victrola. From the Web site Nipperhead.com, on which photographic reproductions of each page of the 1923 and 1924 catalogs are available.

083 Rainer Maria Rilke. "Gong" (1925), in *Selected Poetry of Rainer Maria Rilke*, bilingual edition, ed. and trans. Stephen Mitchell (New York: Random House, 1984), 282; my translation.

083 "... a moment of eternity." Cook, *Cultural Study of Music*, 208.

099 The music is half a century old. On the "late Romanticism" of Rachmaninoff's style and its key role in *Brief Encounter*, see the first chapter of Peter Franklin's forthcoming *Seeing through Music: Reading Film Scores across the Great Divide*.

108 "... most important changes"; "vibratos, trills." Program note to *Grammaire des rêves*, in Kaija Saariaho, *New Gates*, Mode CD 91 (1999).

CHAPTER FOUR: BUT NOT FOR ME

Some portions of this chapter were published under the same main title in *AAA: Arbeiten aus Anglistik und Amerikanistik* 28 (2003): 5–15. The reprinted material appears here by kind permission of the journal's editor, Bernhard Kettemann (Graz, Austria), and the publisher, Gunter Narr Verlag (Tübingen, Germany).

111 "the most eminent composer." Robert Schumann, *On Music and Musicians*, ed. Konrad Wolff, trans. Paul Rosenfeld (New York: Norton, 1969), 112–14.

113 ". . . the castrati disappear." "The Romantic Song," in Roland Barthes, *The Responsibility of Forms: Critical Essays on Music, Art, and Representation*, trans. Richard Howard (Berkeley: University of California Press, 1991), 287.

114 Better than he knew himself. Friedrich Schleiermacher, "*The Hermeneutics:* Outlines of the 1819 Lectures," part 1, sec. 18, trans. Jan Wojcik and Roland Haas, *New Literary History* 10 (1978): 9, reprinted in Vincent B. Leitch, ed., *The Norton Anthology of Criticism and Theory* (New York: Norton, 2001): 621.

115 Music could do that as well or better. For details pertinent to Schubert, see my *Franz Schubert: Sexuality, Subjectivity, Song* (Cambridge: Cambridge University Press, 1998), 102–3.

116 ". . . one transforms oneself into the other." Schleiermacher, "*The Hermeneutics*," part 2, sec. 6, in *New Literary History*, 14, and *Norton Anthology*, 625.

116 The self in its totality. Barthes, "Listening," in *The Responsibility of Forms*, 254–56.

122 A patient's hysteria. Lisa Feuerzeig, "Heroines in Perversity: Marie Schmith, Animal Magnetism, and the Schubert Circle," *19th-Century Music* 21 (1997): 223–43.

122 "Come over to Schober's . . ." Otto Erich Deutsch, ed., *Schubert: Memoirs by His Friends*, trans. Rosamund Ley and John Nowell (London: Adam and Charles Black, 1958), 137–38; translation slightly modified.

124 Strophic variation. For musical details, see Susan Youens, *Retracing a Winter's Journey: Schubert's Winterreise* (Ithaca: Cornell University Press, 1991), 76–80.

129 The ear was not a passive organ. Søren Kierkegaard, *Either/Or: A Fragment of Life*, trans. Alastair Hannay (London: Penguin Books, 1992), 27. As usual with

Kierkegaard, this statement is meant to seem true from a point of view, in this case aesthetic, that may not be his own.

130 ". . . are cradled into poetry . . ." "Julian and Maddalo," l.545–46, in *Shelley's Poetry and Prose*, ed. Donald H. Reiman and Sharon Powers (New York: Norton, 1977), 125.

130 "What is a poet?" Kierkegaard, *Either/Or*, 43.

131 The world of absorbing particulars. See my *Classical Music and Postmodern Knowledge* (Berkeley: University of California Press, 1995), 143–45, and "'Little Pearl Teardrops': Schubert, Schumann, and the Tremulous Body of Romantic Song," in *Music, Sensation, and Sensuality*, ed. Linda Austern (New York: Garland Press, 2002), 57–74.

131 "Doomed to death . . ." Pierre Bourdieu, "A Lecture on the Lecture" (1982), quoted in Andrea Fraser, "'To quote,' say the Kabyles, 'is to bring back to life,'" *October* 101 (2002): 7.

CHAPTER FIVE: THE GHOST IN THE MACHINE

134 Gilbert Ryle. *The Concept of Mind* (1949; reprint, Chicago: University of Chicago Press, 2000). Ryle meant "the ghost in the machine" to be derogatory; in my usage it is not.

135 A large, unwieldy machine. On the significance of the machinic quality of the nineteenth-century piano and its relation to subjectivity, see Richard Leppert, "Cultural Contradiction, Idolatry, and the Piano Virtuoso: Franz Liszt," in *Piano Roles: A New History of the Piano*, ed. James Parakilas (New Haven: Yale University Press, 2002), 200–223.

135 The attitudes of a specific type of self. The role of music in the history of subjectivity is a topic in which I have long

shared an interest with Susan McClary. For recent examples of her approach, see her *Conventional Wisdom: The Content of Musical Form* (Berkeley: University of California Press, 2000) and *Modal Subjectivities: Self-Fashioning in the Italian Madrigal* (Berkeley: University of California Press, 2004).¹

137 Part of a séance. For more on this topic, and pianistic subjectivity in general, see chaps. 2 and 5 of my *Musical Meaning: Toward a Critical History* (Berkeley: University of California Press, 2004), 29–50, 68–99.

143 Make the keys bleed. From Heinrich Heine, "Florentine Nights," in *Poetry and Prose of Heinrich Heine*, ed. and trans. Frederic Ewen (New York: Citadel Press, 1948), 634. The recent literature on Lisztian virtuosity is substantial. In addition to the chapters by Richard Leppert and myself, cited above, see Dana Gooley, *The Virtuoso Liszt* (Cambridge: Cambridge University Press, 2004); Jim Samson, *Virtuosity and the Musical Work: The Transcendental Studies of Liszt* (Cambridge: Cambridge University Press, 2003); and Derek B. Scott, *From the Erotic to the Demonic: On Critical Musicology* (Oxford: Oxford University Press, 2003), 128–54.

143 Filippo Marinetti. "Founding and Manifesto of Futurism 1909," in *Modernism: An Anthology of Sources and Documents*, ed. Vassilki Kolocotroni, Jane Goldman, and Olga Taxidou (Chicago: University of Chicago Press, 1998), 251.

143 *Owl's Clover.* From pt. 4, "A Duck for Dinner," in Wallace Stevens, *Opus Posthumous* (New York: Knopf, 1957), 62.

144 Moments of "bedazzlement." Olivier Messiaen, *Lecture at Notre-Dame* (Paris: Leduc, 2001).

145 "four of his wildest children." Robert Schumann, *On Music and Musicians*, ed. Konrad Wolff, trans. Paul Rosenfeld (New York: Norton, 1969), 140.

149 Evocations of a serenade. On the vocal character of the nocturne, see chap. 2 of Jeffrey Kallberg, *Chopin at the Boundaries: Sex, History, and Musical Genre* (Cambridge, MA: Harvard University Press, 1996), 30–61.

152 "death dances, St. Vitus dances." Robert Schumann, *Jugendbriefe* [Youthful Letters] (Leipzig: Breitkopf and Härtel, 1910), 272.

155 "'That's by him, all right!'"; "'This is by Frédéric Chopin.'" Schumann, *On Music and Musicians*, both 138 (translation of the first quotation slightly modified).

159 Bruno Latour. *We Have Never Been Modern*, trans. Catherine Porter (Cambridge, MA: Harvard University Press, 1993).

162 "I lay my ten fingers." György Ligeti, program note to Ligeti, *Works for Piano: Etudes, Musica Reservata*, György Ligeti Edition, no. 3: Sony CD SK62308 (1996); subsequent quotations from the same source.

164 Schumann . . . said it was not music. Schumann, *On Music and Musicians*, 142.

CHAPTER SIX: CRISIS AND MEMORY

171 Horace. From "Mihi est nonum," *Odes*, bk. 4, no. 11.

173 ". . . the wicked Gauls." Maynard Solomon, *Beethoven* (New York: Schirmer, 1977), 204.

174 The precariousness of ordinary life. For more on this topic, with specific reference to the first of the two trios (nicknamed the "Ghost") and the year 1808, see my "Saving the Ordinary: Beethoven's 'Ghost' Trio and the Wheel of History," *Beethoven Forum* 12 (2005): 50–81.

177 The narrative of the *Pastoral* Symphony is far simpler. It does, though, have a complex backstory. For different

versions, see Raymond Knapp, "A Tale of Two Symphonies: Converging Narratives of Divine Reconciliation in Beethoven's Fifth and Sixth," *Journal of the American Musicological Society* 53 (2000): 291–343, and Richard Will, "Time, Morality, and Humanity in Beethoven's *Pastoral* Symphony," *Journal of the American Musicological Society* 50 (1997): 271–329.

177   "... no longer an orchestra." Hector Berlioz, "Rossini's *William Tell*," in *Source Readings in Music History: The Romantic Period*, ed. Oliver Strunk (New York: Norton, 1965), 70–71.

180   Royal Cyclorama. Anonymous, *Description of the Royal Cyclorama or Music Hall* (London: J. Chisman, 1848).

180   Impersonal, amoral force. Susan Neiman, *Evil in Modern Thought: An Alternative History of Philosophy* (Princeton: Princeton University Press, 2002).

188   We like a storm. Immanuel Kant, *Critique of Judgment*, bk. 2, sec. 28, "Nature as Might."

190   The order of art itself. E. M. Forster, "Art for Art's Sake," from *Two Cheers for Democracy* (London: Edward Arnold, 1951), 98–104.

193   They "resonate" with it. *New York Times*, Arts, May 18, 2002, 8. A few years later, the 9/11 connection could be made more candidly. According to Jonathan Prince, the show's creator and one of its executive producers, "The 60s really began with the assassination of J. F. K, just as our era began with 9/11. Back then, like today, we had a Texan in the White House telling an anxious nation that an unpopular war would soon be over." Quoted in Seth Margolis, "The 60's Saga Continues," *New York Times*, Television, January 2–8, 2005, 4.

196   "far-stretching beauteous landscape." "The Return of the Heroes," l.56, in Walt Whitman, *Leaves of Grass*, ed.

Sculley Bradley and Harold W. Blodgett (New York: Norton, 1973), 361. The poem makes a pro forma effort to include the former Confederacy, but the allegiance of its landscapes is plainly to the Union and its extension into the west.

200   Friedrich Schiller. *On the Aesthetic Education of Man* (1795), trans. Reginald Snell (New York: Ungar, 1954).

202   ". . . until fate strikes me." E. M. Forster, "What I Believe," from *Two Cheers for Democracy*, 81.

202   ". . . Fafner will destroy us." Forster, *Two Cheers*, 80. (Forster writes "Fafnir.")

203   "the nicer knowledge"; "closely the ear attends." Wallace Stevens, "The Pure Good of Theory" (1945), in *Collected Poems of Wallace Stevens* (New York: Knopf, 1954), 332.

204   "The Prologues are over." Wallace Stevens, "Asides on the Oboe" (1940), *Collected Poems*, 250.

204   "the willing suspension of disbelief." Samuel Taylor Coleridge, *Biographia Literaria: Literary Life and Opinions*, chap. 14.

CHAPTER SEVEN: PERSEPHONE'S FIDDLE

209   William Wordsworth. "The Solitary Reaper," from *William Wordsworth*, ed. Stephen Gill (Oxford: Oxford University Press, 1984), 319.

211   Bach added in his own hand. Quoted in Michael Marissen, *The Social and Religious Designs of J. S. Bach's Brandenburg Concertos* (Princeton: Princeton University Press, 1995), 113–14.

211   Milton. "At a Solemn Music" (1632–33), line 6, from *Paradise Regained, the Minor Poems, and Samson Agonistes*, ed. Merritt Y. Hughes (New York: Odyssey, 1937), 207.

212   T. S. Eliot. "The Dry Salvages," from *Four Quartets*, in *Collected Poems, 1909–1963* (New York: Harcourt, Brace, and World, 1963).

212   Christopher Smart. "A Song to David," stanza 77, from *The Norton Anthology of English Literature*, 7th ed., 2 vols., ed. M. H. Abrams and Stephen Greenblatt (New York: Norton, 2000), 1:2855–56.

212   The faculty of attention took on new prominence. See Jonathan Crary, *Suspensions of Perception: Attention, Spectacle, and Modern Culture* (Cambridge, MA: MIT Press, 1999), 11–80.

213   "every crossing of the street." Georg Simmel, "The Metropolis in Mental Life" (1903), trans. Edward A. Shils, in *Modernism: An Anthology of Sources and Documents*, ed. Vassilki Kolocotroni, Jane Goldman, and Olga Taxidou (Chicago: University of Chicago Press, 1998), 52.

213   Bach revival. For details, see Walter Frisch, *German Modernism: Music and the Arts* (Berkeley: University of California Press 2005), 138–85

214   ". . . smoothly flowing rhythm." Simmel, "The Metropolis in Mental Life," in *Modernism*, 52.

216   Johann Georg Sulzer. "Expression in Music," from *General Theory of Fine Art* (1771), in *Music and Aesthetics in the Eighteenth and Early Nineteenth Centuries*, ed. and trans. Peter le Huray and James Day (Cambridge: Cambridge University Press, 1988), 99.

219   Mikhail Bakhtin. "Discourse in the Novel" (1934–35), in *The Dialogic Imagination*, ed. Michael Holquist, trans. Caryl Emerson and Michael Holquist (Austin: University of Texas Press, 1981), 342–48.

INDEX

Text: 10/15 Janson
Display: Janson
Compositor: BookComp Inc.
Printer and Binder: Maple-Vail Manufacturing Group